GRADES **3 – 6**

Strategic Writing Conferences

Smart Conversations That Move Young Writers Forward

teacher's guide

CARL ANDERSON

*first*hand

HEINEMANN

DEDICATION:
This series is dedicated to Haskell Anderson, my beautiful boy.

DEDICATED TO TEACHERS

firsthand
An imprint of Heinemann
361 Hanover Street
Portsmouth, NH 03801
firsthand.heinemann.com

Offices and agents throughout the world

Library of Congress Cataloging-in-Publication Data

Anderson, Carl, 1960-
    Strategic writing conferences: smart conversations that move young
writers forward / by Carl Anderson.
        v.   cm.
    Contents: Topics
    ISBN-13: 978-0-325-01201-8 (set)   ISBN-10: 0-325-01201-6 (set)
    ISBN-13: 978-0-325-02629-9 (v. 1)   ISBN-10: 0-325-02629-7 (v. 1)
    ISBN-13: 978-0-325-02630-5 (v. 2)   ISBN-10: 0-325-02630-0 (v. 2)
    ISBN-13: 978-0-325-02631-2 (v. 3)   ISBN-10: 0-325-02631-9 (v. 3)

    1. English language—Composition and exercises—Study and teaching
(Elementary)   2. Creative writing (Elementary education)   I. Title.
    LB1576.A61594 2009
    372.62'3044—dc22
                                                2008034944

Strategic Writing Conferences
Smart Conversations That Move Young Writers Forward
Teacher's Guide
ISBN 13: 978-0-325-02628-9
ISBN 10: 0-325-02628-2

Strategic Writing Conferences
Smart Conversations That Move Young Writers Forward
ISBN 13: 978-0-325-01201-8
ISBN 10: 0-325-01201-6

Printed in the United States of America on acid-free paper
13   12   11   10   09   ML   1   2   3   4   5

Acknowledgements

THANKS, FIRST, to Lucy Calkins, my mentor.

Thanks to Randy Bomer. His book, *Time for Meaning: Crafting Literate Lives in Middle & High School,* and the diagnostic charts it contains, were the original inspiration for this series.

Thanks to Laurie Pessah, my BFF.

Thanks to the Teachers College Reading and Writing Project community, especially Pam Allyn, Janet Angelillo, Grace Chough, Mary Ann Colbert, Kathy Collins, M. Colleen Cruz, Mary Ehrenworth, Amanda Hartman, Ted Kesler, Leah Mermelstein, Lisa Ripperger, Donna Santman, Hannah Schneewind, Kathleen Tolan, and Amy Ludwig VanDerwater.

Thanks to the colleagues I see at conferences and institutes: Katherine Bomer, Ralph Fletcher, Georgia Heard, Ellin Keene, Lester Laminack, Isoke Nia, and Katie Wood Ray.

Thanks to punctuation guru Dan Feigelson, my comrade-in-Dylan-fandom.

Thanks to Artie and Paula Voigt, and Mimi Aronson, of Literacy Support Systems.

Thanks to Liz Phillips, Beth Handman, and the teachers of PS 321 in Brooklyn; Teresa Caccavale and the teachers of PS 45 in Staten Island; Sharon Hill and the teachers of the Manhattan New School; and Mary Baldwin and the teachers of the Lovett School in Georgia.

Thanks to the coaches of All Write!!! in Indiana. Special thanks to Mindy Hoffar and Julia Nixon. Also to Jim Nixon, principal of South Side Elementary School in Kendallville, Indiana, fourth-grade teacher Mark Schutte, and Mark's students, many of whom are featured in the DVD *Carl on Camera: Modeling Strategic Writing Conferences.*

Thanks to the Lakota Local School District in Ohio and the VIEW literacy team for hosting wonderful summer institutes.

Thanks to Angela Dion of Heinemann Speakers, Cherie Bartlett of Heinemann Workshops, and Vicki Boyd of Heinemann Professional Development.

Special thanks to Kate Montgomery. This project grew out of brainstorming sessions with Kate, and her brilliance as an editor is reflected on every single page.

Thanks to Heather Anderson, who has worked tirelessly on this project and whose enthusiastic emails encouraged me to move forward each day.

Thanks to the other members of Heinemann's *first*hand team: Stephanie Levy, Tina Miller, Charles McQuillen, David Stirling, and Steve Bernier.

Thanks to Pip Clews for her beautiful work on the DVDs.

Thanks to designers Jenny Jensen Greenleaf and Jill Shaffer Hammond.

Last, but most important, thanks to my family: my wife, Robin Epstein, and my two children, Anzia and Haskell. The joy that fills our lives energizes me every day. To all three of you, *I love you.*

Strategic Writing Conferences

Smart Conversations That Move Young Writers Forward

 teacher's guide

Contents

Why *Strategic Writing Conferences?*

MANY TEACHERS HAVE discovered that one of the most powerful ways to teach students to be better writers—if not *the* most powerful way—is to sit beside them and confer with them as they write. These one-to-one conversations, commonly called "writing conferences," are a focused, effective method for teaching writing. They allow educators to teach to students' individual needs as writers and are one of the best ways to differentiate writing instruction. Students, in turn, respond well to conferences because the instruction is personalized—and personal.

However, deciding what to teach and how to best teach it in a conference can be challenging. If you're like many teachers, you're sometimes stumped. When you confer, you may be able to identify an area of need, such as choosing topics wisely, organizing writing effectively, using punctuation skillfully, but you're not always sure which strategy or craft technique to teach to address it. Sometimes, even when you know exactly what strategy to teach, you're not confident that you can teach it so that a student will grasp and be able to use it.

Strategic Writing Conferences will help you know *what* and *how* to teach student writers when you confer with them. It is in part a diagnostic guide, offering descriptions of common areas of need in grades 3–6. Some of these areas are typical of students who are beginning writers, such as how to find topics, write a focused draft, or use punctuation consistently, and some pertain to students who are more advanced writers, such as how to write for audiences, make plans for revising, or use punctuation to emphasize part of a sentence.

For each area of need, *Strategic Writing Conferences* provides a corresponding lesson or lessons. Each one names the writing strategy or craft technique for the student, defines what it is and why it's important, and explains how the student can use it in his writing. All the conferences have been field-tested for many years with students in classrooms across the United States—not only by me but by colleagues and teachers with whom I have worked. Adding the *Strategic Writing Conferences* lessons to your teaching repertoire will help you address your own students' individual areas of need as writers.

An Overview of Conferring

YOU MAY HAVE several important questions about writing conferences:

▶ What are the goals of a writing conference?

▶ When should I confer with students about their writing?

▶ What will conferring look like in my classroom?

▶ What are the teaching moves in a writing conference?

▶ What should I teach in a writing conference?

What are the goals of a writing conference?

When you confer with a student, it isn't your job to fix or edit the student's writing. Rather, it's to teach the student *one* writing strategy or technique he can use in a current piece of writing and continue to use in future writing. As you confer, keep in mind Lucy Calkins' wise advice: "[We] are teaching the writer and not the writing. Our decisions must be guided by 'what might help this *writer*' rather than 'what might help this *writing*'" (1994).

When should I confer with students about their writing?

You can have writing conferences anytime students are writing in your classroom. If you use the writing workshop method, you will confer with students as they spend days and even weeks working on a piece of writing. Usually, writing workshop begins with a short minilesson (a whole group lesson), then students work independently on their writing for twenty to thirty minutes. During this independent writing time, circulate around the classroom and confer with students.

If you teach writing by giving assignments or prompts, confer with students during class as they work on those assignments.

You can even confer with students if you are not a writing teacher. As long as students use your class time to work on writing—whether it is reading, math, science, or social studies—you can confer with them.

What will conferring look like in my classroom?

When conferring, you might move from table to table (or desk to desk) to sit next to students as they write. If you decide to confer at students' tables, it is helpful to carry a small "conferring chair" as you move around the classroom. Or you might sit at a "writing conference table" and call students to you one at a time.

During a conference, sit side by side with the student, with her writing in front of both of you. It is best when the conference feels like a conversation, with both you and the student talking and listening to each other. Ask what the student is doing as a writer, compliment what the student is doing well, then teach a writing strategy or technique. Prompt the student to tell you what she is working on and what she needs help with, and at the end of the conference, to describe how she will use the writing strategy you just taught.

Each writing conference is five to seven minutes; therefore, you will probably confer with four or five students in a class period, depending on how much time students have to work independently. After each conference, note on the record-keeping forms any areas of need and the student's progress. This will help you remember the strategy you taught and your ideas for follow-up conferences.

◆ See writing conferences in action on the *Modeling Strategic Writing Conferences* DVD. The conferences with Ivan (Book 1: *Topics*, Conference 4), Kansas (Book 2: *Drafts*, Conference 24), and Haley (Book 3: *Finished Projects*, Conference 17) are good to watch first.

◆ See pages 13–14 of the *Strategic Writing Conferences Teacher's Guide* for sample record-keeping forms.

What are the teaching moves in a writing conference?

The First Part of the Writing Conference: Identifying the Student's Needs

During the first part of the conference, identify an area of need. First, find out the stage of the writing process the student is in—prewriting (or rehearsal), drafting, revising, or editing—and the specific kind of writing work she is doing at this stage. Then assess how well the student is doing that writing work. For example, the student may be in the prewriting stage, trying to find a topic to write about, but is having trouble finding a really good topic. Or the student may be drafting, trying to write with detail, but her writing is general and does not render a clear picture of the subject. Or the student may be editing by reading her draft to herself, but this strategy isn't helping her locate the end of sentences that need periods.

To identify an area of need, you can take three steps during the first part of the conference.

Step 1: **Ask an open-ended question.** By asking an open-ended question, you invite the student to tell you about what he's doing as a writer. Questions such as "How's it going?" "What are you doing as a writer today?" and "How can I help you today?" are good ones to start with.

Step 2: **Ask follow-up questions.** Once your conversation with the student gets started, ask follow-up questions. Although the best questions can't be planned—you will think of them as you listen to the student tell you what he's doing—there are a few general questions that can help move along a conference. Effective follow-up questions include "Where are you in the writing process?"; "What strategies are you using in this stage of the writing process?"; and "What are you doing to write this piece well?"

Step 3: Look at the student's writing. Looking at the student's writing helps you identify an area of need. Usually it isn't necessary to read an entire notebook entry or draft. If a student is drafting, for example, and working on a lead, just read the lead. If the student is working on topic sentences in a nonfiction draft, take a close look at those sentences.

By the end of the first part of a writing conference, you've identified the area of need. The next step is to use the Diagnostic Guides in *Strategic Writing Conferences* (pages 19–25) to find corresponding conferences.

The Second Part of the Writing Conference: Teaching the Writing Strategy or Craft Technique

In the second part of the writing conference, you'll teach the student a writing strategy or craft technique to help him grow as a writer. *Strategic Writing Conferences* shows you how—clearly and effectively. Every conference models the instructional language and moves that will help you teach students, following these four steps:

Step 1: Give feedback. Preface your teaching by giving the student feedback. Try to point out something the student is doing well—and also name the area of need.

Step 2: Teach. Just like a story reaches the climax, a conference builds to the teaching moment. Your success in helping a student grow as a writer in a conference depends on your skill as a teacher in the next few minutes.

Start by *naming* and *defining* the specific strategy or craft technique that you intend to teach. Explain *why* it's important for the student to learn. To help the student understand the strategy or technique, you might show an example of how a children's book author, such as Patricia Polacco, uses the strategy or technique. Or show how you use the strategy in your own writing. Most importantly, explain *how* the student can use the strategy or technique in his own writing.

Step 3: Try it. Before you end the conference, help the student try the strategy or technique you just taught. Gently nudge the student to talk out how he could use the strategy in his writing, or have the student try it in writing. The purpose of the "try

◆ As you watch the model conferences on the *Carl on Camera: Modeling Strategic Writing Conferences* DVD, notice each teaching step.

◆ For an extended discussion of the teaching steps, watch the *Carl on Camera: Introducing Strategic Writing Conferences* DVD, Part 3, "The Teacher's Role in a Writing Conference," or read *How's It Going? A Practical Guide to Conferring with Student Writers* (Anderson, 2000), Chapters 1 and 2.

it" step is to give the student a taste of the strategy—enough so that you know he is ready to try it independently.

Step 4: Link to the student's work. End the conference by linking the conference to the student's work, that is, tell the student you expect him to try the strategy in his writing and that you hope he will continue to use it in future writing.

With that, the conference is over. Take a minute to jot down some notes about the conference on a record-keeping form. Then you're off to the next conference!

What should I teach in a writing conference?

There are many things students need to learn in order to become lifelong writers—and you can teach them as you confer with students across the school year. *Strategic Writing Conferences* shows how to teach the broad range of writing strategies and techniques students need, including the writing process, qualities of good writing, and how to be initiators of writing.

The **writing process** itself is the focus of many conferences. Students need a repertoire of strategies to help them prewrite (or rehearse a topic before drafting), draft, revise, and edit. You'll find conferences that focus on teaching the writing process in all three books of *Strategic Writing Conferences*. For example, for students who are prewriting, you can teach the strategy of brainstorming topics (Book 1: *Topics,* Conference 1, "Finding a Topic by Making a List"). For students who are drafting, you can teach the strategy of making a plan or outline (Book 2: *Drafts,* Conference 5, "Getting Started by Making a Basic Plan"). For students who are revising, you can teach the strategy of rereading a draft to add details (Book 3: *Finished Projects,* Conference 1, "Revising by Adding Text"). For students who are editing, you can teach the strategy of reading aloud a draft in order to add punctuation (Book 3: *Finished Projects,* Conference 17, "Editing for Clarity by Reading Aloud").

You'll focus many conferences on the **qualities of good writing** and how students can incorporate these qualities into their writing. You'll find conferences that focus on teaching the qualities of good writing in Book 2: *Drafts* and Book 3: *Finished Projects.* For example, you can teach students how to write a focused draft that gets their point across (Book 2: *Drafts,* Conference 6, "Getting Started by Focusing a Bed-to-Bed Story"), teach them how to write precise details (Book 2: *Drafts,* Conference 21, "Crafting a Scene with

◆ For an extended discussion of what to focus on in conferences, read *Assessing Writers* (Anderson, 2004), especially chapters two through five, or watch the DVD *Carl on Camera: Introducing Strategic Writing Conferences* DVD, Part 4, "Assessment of Student Writing."

Precise Details: Actions, Dialogue, and Thoughts"), and how to punctuate sentences to give voice to their writing (Book 3: *Finished Projects,* Conference 13, "Editing for Voice by Using Exclamations and Ellipses").

You can also focus conferences on teaching students how to be **initiators of writing;** that is, to be writers who write purposefully and by choice. Initiators of writing know how to find appropriate audiences for their writing. For example, you can teach students how to identify an appropriate audience, such as specific classmates, for their writing (Book 2: *Drafts,* Conference 1, "Writing with Classmates as an Audience").

Model Texts in Conferences

As you review the conferences in *Strategic Writing Conferences,* you'll notice that most of them include model texts. Some of these model texts are excerpts from children's literature; others are excerpts from my writer's notebook or drafts of pieces I wrote.

It's crucial to show the student model texts during the conference. Model texts help the student "see" what it looks like when a writer uses a strategy or craft technique. It helps the student envision putting the strategy in practice in her own writing. Also, when you use a model text, you are providing guided practice with what Frank Smith (1988) and Katie Ray (1999) call "reading like a writer." When a writer reads work by other writers, she notices the strategies and craft techniques used, then tries the same technique in her own writing. When model texts are used routinely in conferences,

students learn that they, too, can learn from other writers—something they can do for the rest of their lives.

Whenever a conference includes a model text, have the excerpt handy before you confer with the student. To help you prepare for your conferences, each model text is embedded in the conference at point of use, so you can read when and how to use it. The model text is also included as a reproducible at the end of the conference. Of course, when you are using an excerpt of a published piece of children's literature that you have access to, feel free to show the excerpt in the text itself. Many of the model texts are well-known children's books, which can be found in most school libraries or bookstores; you may have several of them in your classroom library already. A list of the model texts used in the three conference books is provided in Appendix A. The model texts that are magazine and newspaper articles are provided in full in Appendix B.

When you refer to a model text during a conference, place the text between you and the student so that the student can easily see it. Take the time to read the excerpt aloud, and ask the student to follow along as you read. (Read the excerpt aloud even if you've already read the whole text or an excerpt to the class during read-aloud time or a minilesson. Writers often read a favorite text over and over when they are studying a technique.) As you teach, point to the features of the text that illustrate what you're explaining so that the student matches your teaching to the appropriate part of the text.

Not only will the conferences in *Strategic Writing Conferences* help you teach writing strategies and techniques with more clarity and precision, they will help you become more comfortable in gen-

eral with the method of using model texts to teach—an important skill for every writing teacher.

Record-Keeping Forms

Like a doctor takes notes about a patient after an examination, a teacher takes notes about a student after a writing conference. These notes will help you anticipate what a student will most likely need to focus on in future conferences. They will help you use *Strategic Writing Conferences* more efficiently and wisely.

There are many kinds of record-keeping forms you can use to take notes and record important information about a conference. Two are included as reproducibles: one is a grid of students in a class, the other is a form to use for individual students. Use these or find another that fits your style and needs as a teacher.

Grid of Students

One of the simplest forms to take notes on is a grid. Use the reproducible that follows, or simply divide a sheet of paper into a series of boxes, one for each student in your class. Put a photocopy of the grid on a clipboard that you carry as you circulate around the room. Jot down notes as you confer with students, including:

▶ today's date and the student's name,
▶ what the student is working on,
▶ your teaching point, and
▶ an area of need that you want to focus on in a future conference.

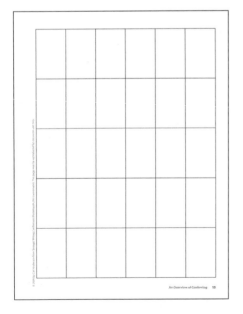

After you have conferred with all the students in your class and filled up the grid, put a blank one on top of your clipboard for the next round of conferences.

How can this form help you? When it's time to confer again with a student, read over your notes from the last conference or two. Your notes will help you anticipate and plan what to teach in the next conference. You may want to revisit the same teaching point again with a student—if you see that he needs further support with it—or you may want to address an area of need that you noted previously but didn't respond to in a previous conference.

Individual Student Form

Another form you may want to use is the "two-column" form. On it, you can record notes from several conferences with *one* student. Teachers who use this form usually have a sectioned binder, with one section for each student in their class. In each student's section are several copies of the form, which provide enough space to take notes for a student across the entire school year.

Record the student's name at the top. Then in the left column, take notes for the conference, including:

▶ today's date,

▶ what the student is working on, and

▶ your teaching point.

In the right column, jot down:

▶ your goals for future writing conferences, such as an area of need you may need to address again and/or areas of need that you haven't yet addressed.

I note my teaching point with a "T" and instructional goal with a "G" to make scanning the form before future conferences easier. Teachers who use the two-column form like how it provides more space to jot down their thoughts about a student after a conference. And when they confer with a student again, it's easy to skim the right column to see what areas of need may come up in the conference.

Whatever record-keeping form you use, your notes can help you use *Strategic Writing Conferences* effectively. After reviewing your notes from previous conferences and identifying the student's areas of need, you may decide to consult the Diagnostic Guides (see pages 19–25) and read through the corresponding conferences in *Strategic Writing Conferences* to prepare for your next conference with

the student. Perhaps you want to find a conference with a teaching point you've already taught but want to revisit, or perhaps you've identified an area of need that you've not yet addressed and want to find a model conference to help you address it. In either case, *Strategic Writing Conferences* can help you imagine how to do the conference well.

As you review your notes, you will probably discover that several students have the same areas of need. If this is the case, meet with these students in a small group. Before gathering the students, consult the conference books—you can use the teaching points in the conferences with small groups as successfully as you can with individual students.

Assessment Notes for _____ Date _____

What am I learning about this student as a writer?	What do I need to teach this student?

(T) is the symbol for Teaching Point.   (G) is the symbol for Instructional Goal.

© 2005 by Carl Anderson from *Assessing Writers*. Heinemann: Portsmouth, NH.

How to Use *Strategic Writing Conferences*

Components of Strategic Writing Conferences

The Conference Books

The three conference books that comprise *Strategic Writing Conferences* contain over one hundred writing lessons. The conferences are organized by stage of writing process (prewriting, drafting, revising, and editing).

▶ Book 1: *Topics.* The Book 1 conferences focus on the prewriting, or rehearsal, stage of the writing process. Conferences focus on how to find topics to write about, explore topics in a writer's notebook, and select and develop topics before drafting.

▶ Book 2: *Drafts.* The Book 2 conferences focus on the *drafting* stage of the writing process. Conferences focus on how to identify an audience for a piece of writing, plan drafts, and craft writing in narrative, fiction, and nonfiction genres.

▶ Book 3: *Finished Projects.* The Book 3 conferences focus on the *revising* and *editing* stages of the writing process. Conferences focus on revision and editing strategies, as well as rules of grammar and mechanics.

The DVDs

Strategic Writing Conferences includes two companion DVDs:

▶ *Carl on Camera: Introducing Strategic Writing Conferences* DVD contains a two-hour workshop on the fundamentals of conferring with student writers.

▶ *Carl on Camera: Modeling Strategic Writing Conferences* DVD models selected conferences from the three conference books.

Using the Conference Books

There are several scenarios in which Book 1: *Topics,* Book 2: *Drafts,* and Book 3: *Finished Projects* will be invaluable to you.

Scenario 1. You are reading a student's writer's notebook or draft and identify an area of need to address in a writing conference. You consult *Strategic Writing Conferences* to prepare what you will teach in this conference. If you notice that several students have the same area of need, you can turn a strategic writing conference into a small group lesson.

Scenario 2. You are in the midst of a writing conference and identify a student's area of need. By consulting the Diagnostic Guides (see pages 19–25) and then the corresponding conference for that need on the spot—in the midst of the conference—you can teach an appropriate writing strategy immediately.

Scenario 3. You realize that one of your writing conferences didn't get through to a student. You consult *Strategic Writing Conferences* for another way to teach the concept. You meet again with the student and try a new approach.

In all three of these scenarios, you identify the student's area of need *first,* then find a corresponding conference. In this way, *Strategic Writing Conferences* differs from units of study in writing—lessons done sequentially, in the order suggested by the author. *Strategic Writing Conferences* is not sequential. In fact, there is no correct order for the conferences. As long as you are selecting conferences that meet needs you've identified, you're using the resource wisely.

Selecting the Appropriate Conference

The three main books in *Strategic Writing Conferences* are arranged to help you easily locate just the right lesson you need in all three of these scenarios.

Step 1: Identify the stage of the writing process. If the student is pre-writing (or rehearsing), refer to Book 1: *Topics.* If the student is drafting, refer to Book 2: *Drafts,* and if the student is revising or editing, refer to Book 3: *Finished Projects.*

Step 2: Use the Diagnostic Guides to locate the appropriate conference. Once you've selected the appropriate conference book, use the Diagnostic Guide at the beginning of the book to locate the conference you want to teach. Look up the student's area of need in the "What You Find" column. Listed in the "Conferences That Can Help" column are the corresponding conferences that have teaching points that address the student's writing need. The three Diagnostic Guides also appear in this Teacher's Guide on pages 19–25.

What Areas of Need Are Addressed by the Conferences?

Book 1: *Topics*

The Book 1: *Topics* conferences address areas of need that occur as students learn to *prewrite* (or *rehearse* their writing) effectively:

▶ "Part 1: Finding Topics" provides conferences that help you teach strategies for finding topics for writing.

▶ "Part 2: Exploring Topics" offers conferences that show students how to explore or "collect" topics in their writer's notebook by writing short entries. By exploring topics, students get a sense of which ones they want to write about as formal drafts for publication. Students often explore topics during the first week of a unit of study and then pick one as a seed topic for a draft. Students may continue to explore topics in their writer's notebook even when they're writing a draft. They may select some of these entries as seed topics later in the school year.

▶ "Part 3: Developing Topics" contains conferences for teaching students how to thoughtfully choose a seed topic to write about as a draft for publication and conferences for developing narrative and nonfiction topics before drafting.

Book 2: *Drafts*

The Book 2: *Drafts* conferences address areas of need that occur when students are learning to *draft* narrative and nonfiction pieces:

▶ "Part 1: Thinking about Audience" provides conferences that teach students how to identify appropriate audiences for their drafts and how to write with those audiences in mind.

▶ "Part 2: Getting Started" contains conferences that teach students how to plan narrative and nonfiction drafts.

▶ "Part 3: Crafting Leads" offers conferences that teach students how to write many kinds of narrative and nonfiction leads.

▶ "Part 4: Crafting Narrative Scenes" provides conferences that teach students how to write narrative scenes with precise detail.

▶ "Part 5: Crafting Nonfiction Sections" teaches students how to write logically organized, precisely detailed sections of nonfiction drafts.

▶ "Part 6: Crafting Endings" contains conferences that teach students how to write narrative and nonfiction endings.

Book 3: *Finished Projects*

The Book 3: *Finished Projects* conferences address areas of need that occur when students are learning to *revise* and *edit*:

▶ "Part 1: Revising" offers conferences that teach revision strategies.

▶ "Part 2: Editing for Voice and Tone" contains conferences that teach students how to edit their writing to create voice and tone.

▶ "Part 3: Editing for Clarity" offers conferences that teach students editing strategies, as well as grammar and mechanics.

▶ "Part 4: Planning Writing Beyond the School Year" contains conferences that teach students how to continue writing after the school year.

In some parts, several conferences address the same area of need. For example, "Part 3: Crafting Leads" in Book 2: *Drafts* contains seven conferences. In these cases, the conferences are arranged in order of increasing difficulty. The first in the section is designed for a novice writer; the later ones, for the more advanced writer. Having a selection of conferences to choose from helps you differentiate your teaching to better address the needs of students at different levels.

Diagnostic Guide for Book 1: *Topics*

The Diagnostic Guide is designed to help you locate a conference that addresses a student's particular area of need. The guide lists areas of need that a student may have when he's finding, exploring, selecting, and developing topics.

Part One: Finding Topics

WHAT YOU FIND	CONFERENCES THAT CAN HELP	
The student...		**Page**
... is having trouble generating ideas for notebook entries or drafts.	1. Making a List ✳	7
	2. Reading the World	12
	3. Free Writing	17
	4. Brainstorming Writing Territories ✳	22
... abandons a writing territory after writing about it only once or twice.	5. Mining a Writing Territory ✳	26
... has several favorite topics, but he's tired of writing about them.	6. Updating Writing Territories	35
... doesn't know much about a new topic he's eager to write about.	7. Turning an Unfamiliar Topic into a Writing Territory	39

Part Two: Exploring Topics

WHAT YOU FIND	CONFERENCES THAT CAN HELP	
The student...		**Page**
... has uninspired entries in his writer's notebook.	8. "Unpacking" One Moment ✳	47
	9. Visualizing and Talking	51
... is writing entries that are focused on the object or hobby rather than on the writer's experiences with it.	10. Adding Yourself ✳	54
... isn't sure how to write entries that support nonfiction writing.	11. Writing about Facts and Questions	58
... isn't sure how to write entries that support fiction writing.	12. Writing about a Character	68
... writes about topics in the same way all the time.	13. Writing in a Variety of Ways	72

A conference with an ✳ is one of Carl's Classics.

Part Three: Developing Topics

Diagnostic Guide for Book 2: *Drafts*

The Diagnostic Guide is designed to help you locate a conference that addresses a student's particular area of need. The guide lists areas of need that a student may have when she's thinking about audience; getting started with a draft; and crafting leads, narrative scenes, nonfiction sections, and endings.

Part One: Thinking about Audience

WHAT YOU FIND	CONFERENCES THAT CAN HELP	
The student...		**Page**
... doesn't have a clear idea of the audience for his piece.	1. Writing with Classmates as an Audience ✶	9
... has written a piece that would appeal to an audience beyond his circle of friends, relatives, and acquaintances inside and outside of school.	2. Writing with Community Members as an Audience	12
	3. Writing with Print or Online Readers as an Audience	15

Part Two: Getting Started

WHAT YOU FIND	CONFERENCES THAT CAN HELP	
The student...		**Page**
... is drafting a story without making a plan, but the draft is undeveloped and the parts may be in an order that doesn't make sense.	4 Talking Out a Story	19
	5. Making a Basic Plan ✶	23
... has written a "bed-to-bed" or "all-about" entry (an entry in which a student tells *every* detail that she can remember about an experience).	6. Focusing a Bed-to-Bed Story ✶	27
	7. Using a Timeline	30
... has made a story plan that includes several scenes but that lacks details.	8. Writing a Detailed Plan	34
... is confused about how to proceed from a seed entry about a fictional character to a draft of a fictional story.	9. Thinking about a Story's Problem and Solution	38
... has written a plan for a story but has included unnecessary scenes and/or may need to include additional scenes. He hasn't indicated which scenes are especially important to the story.	10. Revising a Plan	42

A conference with an ✶ is one of Carl's Classics.

… has written all of her previous stories in first person because she can't imagine doing otherwise, not because she has weighed the pros and cons of this choice.	11. Telling a Story in First or Third Person	46
… has developed her topic for a nonfiction piece in her notebook but is confused about how to begin writing her draft.	12. Planning Nonfiction Across Several Pages	51
	13. Writing a Flowchart for Nonfiction	54

Part Three: Crafting Leads

WHAT YOU FIND	CONFERENCES THAT CAN HELP	
The student…		**Page**
… is writing a story that starts with a scene that is not essential to the story.	14. Starting with an Important Scene ✳	63
… has started with a scene that's essential to the story, but this first scene lacks tension or interest because it doesn't establish the problem or conflict, include information about the characters, or describe the setting.	15. Creating Tension	67
	16. Writing Character Background	71
	17 Describing the Setting	77
… introduces the reader to his nonfiction topic in his lead, but not the point he is going to make about it.	18. Basic Nonfiction Lead	83
… can write basic nonfiction leads but doesn't yet have other kinds of nonfiction leads in his repertoire.	19. Writing a Scene for Nonfiction	87
	20. Writing a Comparison for Nonfiction	93

Part Four: Crafting Narrative Scenes

WHAT YOU FIND	CONFERENCES THAT CAN HELP	
The student…		**Page**
… is beginning to write focused narratives but has written mostly general details.	21. Precise Details: Actions, Dialogue, and Thoughts ✳	99
	22. Writing Dialogue	103
	23. Showing—and Telling—Character Feelings and Thoughts	107
	24. Describing Character Actions	111
… uses the basic repertoire of narrative details in his writing—character actions, dialogue, character thoughts and feelings—and can grow by adding other kinds of details to his repertoire.	25. Using Defining Details to Create a Vivid Character	115
	26. Weaving in Setting Details	120
… writes using general words in his stories that make it hard to "see" a detailed picture of the characters, setting, and events.	27. Using Exact Words ✳	126
	28. Using Simile	131
… relies heavily on the transition "then" to signal changes between and within scenes.	29. Using Time Transitions ✳	138
… develops every scene in his story, even ones that don't play a crucial role.	30. Summarizing—Not Stretching—a Scene	143

Part Five: Crafting Nonfiction Sections

WHAT YOU FIND	CONFERENCES THAT CAN HELP	
The student...		**Page**
... is writing a section that is a series of details but lacks a topic sentence that gives an overview of the section.	31. Topic and Detail Sentences	149
... writes about a topic that will be unfamiliar to the intended audience.	32. Defining Unfamiliar Terms	154
	37. Writing a Background Section	177
... is unsure of how to use the material she gathered in an interview effectively in her draft.	33. Quoting Experts	158
... writes with an impersonal tone, similar to an encyclopedia entry.	34. Giving Voice to Nonfiction by Addressing the Reader	162
	35. Giving Voice to Nonfiction by Commenting on Facts	166
... writes without using transitions from section to section, and consequently his draft is confusing to readers.	36. Using Paragraphs and Headings	171
... is writing a draft that would benefit from a narrative procedure ("how-to") section.	38. Writing a How-To Section	182
... has developed a point in a nonfiction piece with a narrative section, but the section is too long and overwhelms the piece.	39. Writing a Mini-Narrative Section	185

Part Six: Crafting Endings

WHAT YOU FIND	CONFERENCES THAT CAN HELP	
The student...		**Page**
... has ended with a scene that doesn't seem connected to the meaning of the story or has ended without communicating meaning explicitly.	40. Writing a Scene That's Integral to the Story ✳	193
	41. Writing a Reflection	197
... doesn't know how to end nonfiction pieces, and has ended his piece superficially or awkwardly.	42. Leaving the Reader Thinking	202
	43. Connecting to the Reader's Life	206

Diagnostic Guide for Book 3: *Finished Projects*

The Diagnostic Guide is designed to help you locate a conference that addresses a student's particular area of need. The guide lists areas of need that a student may have when he's revising, editing, and planning his writing after the school year is over.

Part One: Revising

WHAT YOU FIND	CONFERENCES THAT CAN HELP	
The student...		**Page**
...has made few or no revisions to his draft.	1. Adding Text ✳	5
	2. Using Blank Pages, Sticky Notes, "Spider Legs," and "Add Ons" ✳	13
...has written a story in which she retells everything that happened during an event or a nonfiction piece in which she tells every single fact she knows about her topic.	3. Focusing an "All About" Story✳	18
...has revised his draft by adding text, but the parts that he's added onto are not the most important parts in the piece.	4. Focusing on Important Scenes ✳	21
...has written a draft that is confusing due to the order of its scenes or the inclusion of scenes that have little to do with the central message.	5. Reordering the Scenes or Sections	26
	6. Cutting Scenes or Sections	29
...has used general, inexact words in his draft or title.	7. Using a Thesaurus and Dictionary	31
	10. Writing an Effective Title	46
...has plunged into revising her draft without taking time to consider which parts are revision priorities or if a new meaning can be developed.	8. Making a Comprehensive Revision Plan	36
	9. Developing a New Meaning	41
...has been working with a partner to revise a draft, but they are confused about how to give and receive feedback.	11. Using Feedback from a Partner ✳	51

A conference with an ✳ is one of Carl's Classics.

Part Two: Editing for Voice and Tone

WHAT YOU FIND	CONFERENCES THAT CAN HELP	
The student...		**Page**
. . . emphasizes certain words, phrases, or sentences when he reads a draft aloud but hasn't signaled to readers to do this when they read.	12. Adding Italics or Full Caps	57
	13. Using Exclamations and Ellipses	61
	14. Using the Dash to Create Emphasis	65
. . . has overused punctuation marks in her draft such as the exclamation mark, ellipsis, or dash.	15. Using Punctuation Judiciously	69
. . . has created a tone in his draft through choice of words that does not match the intended audience or purpose of the draft.	16. Choosing Words	71

Part Three: Editing for Clarity

WHAT YOU FIND	CONFERENCES THAT CAN HELP	
The student...		**Page**
. . . has made little attempt to edit her draft or has edited her draft by reading it to himself and numerous errors remain in it.	17. Reading Aloud ✳	77
	18. Using Feedback from a Partner ✳	80
	19. Using a Checklist ✳	82
. . . has written a draft in which he has used ending punctuation inconsistently, or not at all.	20. Listening for Pauses ✳	85
. . . . has written a draft that primarily uses simple sentences, rarely compound sentences.	21. Creating and Punctuating Compound Sentences	90
. . . . has written a draft that overuses the word **and.**	22. Deleting *"and"*	94
. . . has incorrectly punctuated dialogue or complex sentences.	23. Punctuating Dialogue	98
	24. Checking for Sentence Fragments	102
. . . has not used paragraphs consistently in his draft.	25. Creating Paragraphs ✳	106
. . . has sentences that lack clarifying details or short sentences that could be combined.	26. Adding Details Inside a Sentence	112

Part Four: Planning Writing Beyond the School Year

WHAT YOU FIND	CONFERENCES THAT CAN HELP	
The student...		**Page**
. . . is unsure of how to continue learning about craft and writing after the school year is over.	27. Making a Writing Plan for the Future	119
	28. Reading Like a Writer with a Self-Chosen Author	123

Conference Walkthrough

Every conference in Books 1–3 shows you how to teach a specific writing strategy, craft technique, or point of grammar or mechanics. The predictable features of each conference model a framework for teaching a student effectively. In addition, marginal notes offer coaching, background information, and/or ideas for modifying the conference.

The first four sections help you prepare for the conference:

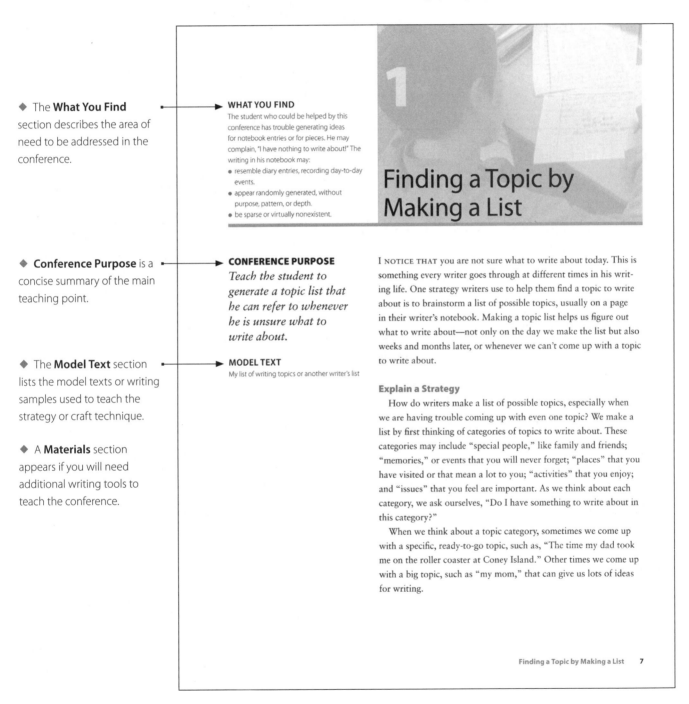

◆ The **What You Find** section describes the area of need to be addressed in the conference.

◆ **Conference Purpose** is a concise summary of the main teaching point.

◆ The **Model Text** section lists the model texts or writing samples used to teach the strategy or craft technique.

◆ A **Materials** section appears if you will need additional writing tools to teach the conference.

WHAT YOU FIND
The student who could be helped by this conference has trouble generating ideas for notebook entries or for pieces. He may complain, "I have nothing to write about!" The writing in his notebook may:
● resemble diary entries, recording day-to-day events.
● appear randomly generated, without purpose, pattern, or depth.
● be sparse or virtually nonexistent.

Finding a Topic by Making a List

CONFERENCE PURPOSE
Teach the student to generate a topic list that he can refer to whenever he is unsure what to write about.

MODEL TEXT
My list of writing topics or another writer's list

I NOTICE THAT you are not sure what to write about today. This is something every writer goes through at different times in his writing life. One strategy writers use to help them find a topic to write about is to brainstorm a list of possible topics, usually on a page in their writer's notebook. Making a topic list helps us figure out what to write about—not only on the day we make the list but also weeks and months later, or whenever we can't come up with a topic to write about.

Explain a Strategy

How do writers make a list of possible topics, especially when we are having trouble coming up with even one topic? We make a list by first thinking of categories of topics to write about. These categories may include "special people," like family and friends; "memories," or events that you will never forget; "places" that you have visited or that mean a lot to you; "activities" that you enjoy; and "issues" that you feel are important. As we think about each category, we ask ourselves, "Do I have something to write about in this category?"

When we think about a topic category, sometimes we come up with a specific, ready-to-go topic, such as, "The time my dad took me on the roller coaster at Coney Island." Other times we come up with a big topic, such as "my mom," that can give us lots of ideas for writing.

Finding a Topic by Making a List　**7**

The conference teaching language begins after these four sections. It models how to begin a conference by offering feedback to the student. It shows how to talk about the area of need and name and define the writing strategy, craft technique, or point of grammar or mechanics that you will teach. The teaching language is followed by five sections:

◆ The **Explain a Strategy** section offers a clear, explicit explanation of how writers use a writing strategy.

◆ **Share Your Writing** models how to use your own piece of writing to teach a strategy, technique, or point of grammar or mechanics.

◆ The **Share a Model Text** section models how to teach an aspect of writer's craft using an excerpt from children's literature or a nonfiction piece. You can use the models provided or try one of your favorites.

◆ The **Coach the Student** section gives you scaffolding questions to help you guide the student to try what you've just taught.

◆ **Link to the Student's Writing** shows how to wrap up the conference. It models how to explain what you would like the student to do *right now* in his own writing and helps you summarize the teaching point.

Topics I Can Write About

* the time dad showed me the newborn baby rabbits
* riding the waves at Robert Moses State Park with my sisters
* the time we went clamming in Cape Cod
* launching model rockets at Tobay Beach
* winning my first sailboat race
* when Adrian bullied me after my class beat his in a spelling bee

◆ Suggest a category to the student, based on what you know about him. For example, if you know a student went fishing with her brother recently, you might say, "I'm sure you've got some good ideas in the category 'family.' What about when you went fishing with your brother this past weekend?"

Share Your Writing

I want to show you my own list of topics that I brainstormed in my writer's notebook based on categories.

I started to write this list by thinking of the topic category "family." As I thought about this category, I came up with a few important experiences that I shared with my family, such as "the time my dad showed me the newborn baby rabbits" and "riding the waves at Robert Moses State Park with my sisters."

Then I thought of the topic category "places." As I thought about places that mean a lot to me, or did when I was a kid, I came up with the idea "the time we went clamming in Cape Cod." Then I continued to think of different topic categories, and brainstormed even more ideas for writing.

Coach the Student

I'd like to help you use categories to brainstorm a list of possible topics you could write about.

▶ Is there a category you would like to think about first? What can you write about in this category?

▶ What about the topic category "family"? Are there special people in your family that you would like to write about? What experiences or special moments with your family come to mind that you might write about?

▶ What about other topic categories—"friends," "places," "issues"?

Link to the Student's Writing

I'd like you to make a list of topics right now in your writer's notebook that you will draw ideas from to write about. To help you do this, I'm going to give you a list of topic categories (see page 11) that you can look at as you make the list.

Remember that whenever you're stuck for a topic to write about, you can make a list of possible topics by thinking about categories. The list you make can help you find a topic to write about now and also give you topics to write about in the future.

In addition to these sections, which form the bulk of the conference, three sections sometimes appear, which provide further information:

◆ The **Follow-Up** section gives ideas for modifying the conference during subsequent units of study and/or ideas for additional conferences about the same topic.

◆ **Modifications for Nonfiction Genres** provides guidelines for adapting the conference for use with students who are writing in nonfiction genres.

◆ A **Sources** section appears when applicable that shares the inspiration for the conference and provides references to the professional literature.

FOLLOW-UP

▶ Later on in the year, when your class is studying a genre other than narrative, angle the conference toward that genre. For example, if the class is studying feature articles, tell students they can ask themselves, "Is there something I want to teach readers about in this category, activities and hobbies?" If the class is studying op-eds, students can ask, "Do I have opinions about something in this category, issues I feel passionate about?" If the class is studying personal essay, students can ask, "Do I have any ideas about something in this category, memories?"

▶ In a unit of study in which students choose the genre, tell students that they can ask themselves this all-inclusive set of questions: "Do I have a story in this category? Something I want to teach readers about? An opinion? Or an idea?" Angling the conference in this way helps students find ideas for writing in numerous genres.

SOURCES

I learned this strategy from Randy Bomer, who discusses giving kids a list of topic categories to write about in *Time for Meaning* (1995).

I developed many of the conferences in this book by learning from many educators. Lucy Calkins has written extensively about writer's notebooks in *The Art of Teaching Writing* (1994), *Living Between the Lines* (with Shelley Harwayne, 1990), and *Units of Study for Teaching Writing Grades 3-5* (with colleagues, 2006). Randy Bomer's *Time for Meaning* (1995)—which inspired Conference 1—describes teaching middle and high school students to use notebooks as a rehearsal tool. Don Murray's *Write to Learn* (2004), Ralph Fletcher's *Breathing In, Breathing Out* (1996), Aimee Buckner's *Notebook Know-How: Strategies for the Writer's Notebook* (2005), Judy Davis and Sharon Hill's *The No Nonsense Guide to Teaching Writing* (2003) and Ralph Fletcher and JoAnn Portalupi's *Lessons for the Writer's Notebook* (2005) are other invaluable resources.

Carl's "Classic Twenty-Five" Conferences

Twenty-five of the strategic writing conferences are especially important to add to your teaching repertoire. These select conferences address needs that a majority of students have as writers, especially early in the school year when they begin writing. It is likely that you will have these conferences again and again with students during the first few months of school.

Many of these "classic" conferences teach strategies for navigating the stages of the writing process—finding topics, selecting a seed topic, planning a piece, and revising and editing a draft. These strategies are essential for students to learn in order to function independently as writers in your classroom. Some of the conferences teach the basic qualities of effective writing. They help students focus on meaning and write details, improving their current writing project as well as future ones.

Many of the "classic" conferences help students write in narrative genres. Since many writing teachers begin the school year with one or more units of study focused on narrative genres, these "classic" conferences are especially useful at this time.

In addition, many of the "classic" conferences are "firsts." They are the first in a group of conferences that address a particular area of need. For example, Conference 14, "Crafting a Lead by Starting with an Important Scene," is the first of four conferences in Book 2: *Drafts* to teach students to write narrative leads. Once you learn how to conduct this classic conference, you can add the others to your repertoire. This helps you more successfully differentiate your instruction.

Finally, many of the classic conferences end with suggestions to adjust them for students who are writing nonfiction (see "Modifications for Nonfiction Genres" at the end of the conferences). With the classic conferences in your repertoire, learning how to teach these nonfiction conferences won't feel completely new; rather, you'll find that you are learning how to simply adjust a conference to make it work with nonfiction.

As you begin to use *Strategic Writing Conferences,* review the classic conferences first. The classic conferences are listed in the table on the next page. They are also marked in the Diagnostic Guide and the table of contents of each conference book so that you can refer to them easily. With the classic conferences as part of your teaching repertoire, you are equipped to teach students the fundamentals of writing right from the start.

Carl's "Classic Twenty-Five" Conferences

Book 1: *Topics*

Conference Number	Conference Title
1	Finding a Topic by Making a List
4	Finding a Topic by Brainstorming Writing Territories
5	Finding a Topic by Mining a Writing Territory
8	Exploring a Topic by "Unpacking" One Moment
10	Exploring a Topic by Adding Yourself
14	Selecting a Topic by Considering Interest, Audience, or Occasion
16	Developing a Topic by Reflecting on Its Significance

Book 2: *Drafts*

Conference Number	Conference Title
1	Writing with Classmates as an Audience
5	Getting Started by Making a Basic Plan
6	Getting Started by Focusing a Bed-to-Bed Story
14	Crafting a Lead by Starting with an Important Scene
21	Crafting a Scene with Precise Details: Actions, Dialogue, and Thoughts
27	Crafting a Draft by Using Exact Words
29	Crafting a Draft by Using Time Transitions
40	Crafting an Ending by Writing a Scene That's Integral to the Story

Book 3: *Finished Projects*

Conference Number	Conference Title
1	Revising by Adding Text
2	Revising by Using Blank Pages, Sticky Notes, "Spider Legs," and "Add Ons"
3	Revising by Focusing an "All About" Story
4	Revising by Focusing on Important Scenes
11	Revising by Using Feedback from a Partner
17	Editing for Clarity by Reading Aloud
18	Editing for Clarity by Using Feedback from a Partner
19	Editing for Clarity by Using a Checklist
20	Editing for Clarity by Listening for Pauses
25	Editing for Clarity by Creating Paragraphs

Viewing *Carl on Camera: Introducing Strategic Writing Conferences* DVD

THE *Carl on Camera: Introducing Strategic Writing Conferences* DVD contains my professional development workshop that explores the fundamentals of conferring with student writers. You can use the *Carl on Camera: Introducing Strategic Writing Conferences* DVD to learn about conferring before you use *Strategic Writing Conferences* in your classroom. The DVD contains the following parts:

Part 1: Introduction to Writing Conferences
Part 2: Key Concepts for Writing Conferences
- ▶ Conferences Are Conversations
- ▶ Conferences Help Students Become Better Writers
- ▶ Conferences Have a Predictable Structure
- ▶ Show Students That You Care
Part 3: The Teacher's Role in a Writing Conference
Part 4: Assessment of Student Writing
- ▶ Assessment Lenses
- ▶ Traits of Good Writing
- ▶ Exemplar Pieces
- ▶ A Typical Pattern: The "All About" Story
- ▶ Conference Notes and Records
Part 5: Frequently Asked Questions about Conferring

You can also view the workshop as part of a course on the "how to's" of conferring. If you're a teacher, you could take this course yourself. If you're a literacy coach, you might lead this course with teachers you're mentoring or as part of study group or inservice.

Whether you choose self-study or decide to build a course around the workshop, you could watch the entire workshop or go by topic. View just the parts that meet your own specific needs—or the needs shared by the teachers you coach. The following viewing guide to *Carl on Camera: Introducing Writing Conferences* is designed to help you focus on the essential points discussed in the workshop.

Part 1: Introduction to Writing Conferences

Before watching this part, reflect on or discuss these questions:

▶ How are your writing conferences going?

▶ Think about a recent writing conference that you had with a student. What went well in the conference? What would you like to improve?

▶ What do you need to learn to become better at conferring with students about their writing?

Part 2: Key Concepts for Writing Conferences

Before watching this part, get an image in your mind of an effective writing conference. You may want to view one or more of the conferences on the *Carl on Camera: Modeling Strategic Writing Conferences* DVD. In Part 2, I discuss my conference with Brendan (Book 1: *Topics*, Conference 5, "Finding a Topic by Mining a Writing Territory"); this would be a good conference to view first.

After watching each of the following sections, reflect on or discuss these questions:

Conferences Are Conversations

▶ What is the tone of a writing conference?

▶ Why is it important to establish this tone?

▶ What contributes to the tone of a writing conference?

▶ What tone do you usually establish in your writing conferences, and why?

▶ What changes could you make to improve the tone of your conferences?

Conferences Help Students Become Better Writers

▶ What is the goal of a writing conference?

- What does it mean to "teach a child to be a better writer"?
- What is the difference between editing a child's piece of writing and teaching him to be a better writer?
- Are you more of an editor in your conferences or a teacher? If you're more of an editor, what changes could you make to change your goal?

Conferences Have a Predictable Structure

- What is the structure of a writing conference?
- What happens in each part of a writing conference?
- Do your conferences have this structure? If not, what can you start doing in your conferences?

Show Students That You Care

◆ To explore this topic further, read Chapter 1 of *How's It Going? A Practical Guide to Conferring with Student Writers* (Anderson, 2000).

- Why is it important to show students that we care about them as people and writers in writing conferences?
- In what ways can we show students that we care about them as writers?
- What teachers in your life showed interest in you as a writer? What effect did this have on you?
- What can you start doing in your conferences to better communicate that your care about students as people and as writers?

Part 3: The Teacher's Role in a Writing Conference

◆ Refer to the handout "The Roles of Teacher and Student in a Writing Conference" (page 37) when you view this part.

After watching each of the following sections, reflect on or discuss these questions:

Invite the Student to Set an Agenda

- How do we invite a student to set a conference agenda?
- How do you start your conferences?
- Are students regularly telling you what they're doing as writers in the beginning of your conferences? If not, in what other ways could you start your conferences that might invite more student talk?

Ask Research Questions

- What kinds of research questions do we ask?
- How do we generate research questions?
- What kinds of research questions do you regularly ask students?

Are there aspects of writing that you don't usually ask students about? What are they? What questions could you ask to nudge students to talk about these aspects?

Look at the Student's Writing

- How do we look at the student's writing during a conference?
- Do you usually have students read their entire piece aloud, or do you read their entire piece? How could you read student writing more efficiently?

Give Feedback

- What kinds of feedback do we give students in conferences?
- What is the appropriate tone of the feedback?
- What kind of feedback do you usually give students? Do you compliment students for what they're doing well? Do you clearly name what students need to work on to improve as writers?
- In what ways could you improve the tone of your feedback?

Teach the Student

- In what ways can we teach in a conference?
- What are the components of the teaching move? What happens in each of the components?
- In what ways do you typically teach students in conferences?
- Think about your conference teaching moves. Which steps do your teaching moves contain? Which steps could you add to your teaching moves to make them more effective?

Coach the Student

- Why is it important for students to try what we teach them during the conference?
- How can we coach students as they try out what we've taught?
- In what ways could you improve your coaching of students in conferences?

Link to the Student's Work

- What is the purpose of the link?
- How do you bring your own conferences to closure? What else could you do to help students understand what you want them to do after the conference and to continue doing in future pieces of writing?

◆ To explore this topic further, read Chapter 2 of *How's It Going? A Practical Guide to Conferring with Student Writers* (Anderson, 2000).

Part 4: Assessment of Student Writing

After watching each of the following sections, reflect on or discuss these questions:

Assessment Lenses

◆ Refer to the handout "Developing an Assessment Lens" (page 38) when you view this section.

▶ What is a writing pattern?

▶ How does recognizing writing patterns help us decide what to teach?

▶ Why is it important to have a set of assessment lenses?

▶ What is a lifelong writer?

▶ What does it mean to be an initiator of writing?

▶ What does it mean to write well?

▶ What does it mean to have an effective writing process?

▶ What are *your* assessment lenses? What other lenses could you look at students through to help you create a more complete picture of them as writers?

Traits of Good Writing

◆ Refer to the handout "The Traits of Good Writing" (page 39) when you view this section.

▶ What is meaning? Why is it such an important trait?

▶ What is structure?

▶ What is detail?

▶ What is voice?

▶ What are conventions?

▶ Which of these traits are you most comfortable with and regularly assess in students' writing? Which traits are you less comfortable with and need to learn about in order to assess them in students' writing?

Exemplar Pieces

◆ Refer to Abby's and Helaina's pieces (page 40) when you view this section.

▶ Why is it important to study exemplar pieces?

▶ After reading Abby's piece, "When I Went On The Mountain Slide," what did you learn about what she knows about writing well?

▶ After reading Helaina's piece, "What's Up in the Field of Grass?" what did you learn about what she knows about writing well?

A Typical Pattern: The "All About" Story

◆ To learn how to confer with a student who has written an all about story, read Book 3: *Finished Projects*, Conference 3, "Revising by Focusing an 'All About' Story" or watch my conference with Cooper on *Carl on Camera: Modeling Strategic Writing Conferences* DVD.

▶ Why do students write "all about" pieces?

▶ What should we teach students who write "all about" pieces?

▶ What other patterns do you regularly see in students' writing? What do you teach students when you see these patterns?

◆ Refer to my record-keeping form (page 41) when you view this section. You can learn additional information about record keeping and find reproducible record-keeping forms in "An Overview of Conferring" (pages 10–14).

◆ To explore the topic of assessing student writing further, read the following chapters in *Assessing Writers* (Anderson, 2004): If you're interested in learning more about assessment lenses, read Chapters 2–5; the traits of good writing, Chapter 4; or record keeping, Chapter 6.

Conference Notes and Records

❱ How can setting instructional goals for students help you confer with them?

❱ How can keeping records of your conferences help you set up and follow through on your instructional goals for students?

❱ What record-keeping form do you use in conferences? Are you able to record your instructional goals for students in this form?

❱ Is there another form that might help you record your goals for students?

Part 5: Frequently Asked Questions about Conferring

After watching this part, reflect on or discuss these questions:

❱ What are the advantages of conferring with students at their seats? At a special conferring table?

❱ Where do you confer with students? Where else could you confer with students that might create a safer tone in your conferences?

❱ When is the best time in the writing process to confer with students? Why?

❱ When do you confer with students? Is this the most effective time to confer with students, or do you need to rethink this?

❱ What are the advantages of your initiating conferences with students?

❱ Who initiates conferences in your classroom, you or the students? Are you getting to see all of the students in your classroom? If not, what can you do to ensure you confer with all of your students?

❱ What is the average length of conferences?

❱ How long are your conferences? If they regularly go beyond five to seven minutes, what can you do to shorten their length?

Final Discussion Questions

After watching the workshop, reflect on or discuss these questions:

❱ What new understandings of conferring have I gained from this workshop?

❱ How can I take what I learned and apply it to my own writing conferences?

❱ What is the first step I'll take to improve my writing conferences?

The Roles of Teacher and Student in a Writing Conference

THE TEACHER'S ROLE	THE STUDENT'S ROLE
In the first part of the conference:	
◆ Invite the student to set an agenda for the conference.	◆ Set the agenda for the conference by describing her writing work.
◆ Ask assessment questions.	
◆ Read the student's writing.	◆ Respond to the teacher's research questions by describing her writing work more deeply.
◆ Make a teaching decision.	
In the second part of the conference:	
◆ Give the student critical feedback.	◆ Listen carefully to the teacher's feedback and teaching.
◆ Teach the student.	◆ Ask questions to clarify and deepen her understanding of the teacher's feedback and teaching.
◆ Nudge the student to "have a go."	◆ "Have a go" with what the teacher taught.
◆ Link the conference to the student's independent work.	◆ Commit to trying on her own what the teacher taught.

Adapted from *How's It Going? A Practical Guide to Conferring with Student Writers* (Anderson, 2000).

Developing an Assessment Lens

Assessment begins with developing a vision for what you want a student to become as a writer. This vision becomes an assessment lens that helps you sift through information you gather about the student's writing. My vision is that each student will become a lifelong writer. What I look for when I assess a student is how he resembles a lifelong writer.

A lifelong writer demonstrates *initiative* as a writer when he:
 ▶ writes by choice for purposes that matter to him.
 ▶ writes for audiences that matter to him.

A lifelong writer *writes well* when he:
 ▶ communicates meaning in his writing.
 ▶ structures texts in ways that enable the reader to grasp his meaning.
 ▶ uses precise detail to develop parts of the structure.
 ▶ gives his writing an appropriate voice that enhances his meaning.
 ▶ uses conventions to guide the reader through the text and enhance the meaning.

A lifelong writer has a *writing process* that works when he uses:
 ▶ a repertoire of writing strategies to navigate the writing process (prewriting, drafting, revising, and editing).
 ▶ strategies that enable him to write well time and time again.

The Traits of Good Writing

MEANING

◗ *Meaning* is what the author has to say or the "point" she wants to make about the topic.

◗ Meaning influences the decisions the writer makes while composing a text.

◗ Some students see writing as retelling instead of as communicating meaning.

STRUCTURE

◗ *Structure* refers to the parts of a text and the roles and interrelationships of these parts.

◗ The writer's meaning helps her select the structure—which parts to include or focus on. The role of each part is to help develop the writer's meaning.

◗ The writer decides which kinds of parts to include in a text.

◗ In narrative genres, the parts are ordered sequentially (by time); in non-narrative genres, logic binds the parts together.

◗ Leads, endings, and transitions guide the reader to create meaning.

◗ The writer weights some parts more than others because they play a more crucial role in developing meaning.

DETAIL

◗ *Details* are the particulars (or specifics) of a piece of writing.

◗ Every detail plays a role in developing what the writer wants to say about the topic.

◗ The writer uses a range of detail to develop meaning.

◗ Details are composed of specific words that describe exactly what happens in a narrative or that describe exactly the subject of a non-narrative.

VOICE

◗ *Voice* is the writer's presence on the page. It's the sense that there is a person behind the words.

◗ The writer uses voice to enhance her meaning.

◗ The writer creates voice in the way she writes sentences.

◗ The writer creates voice in the way she uses punctuation.

◗ The writer creates voice through choice of detail.

CONVENTIONS

◗ *Conventions* of written English are tools that help the writer communicate meaning.

◗ Students' errors are either careless errors or signs that they are growing as writers.

◗ Students make predictable errors when they are on "syntactic thresholds," that is, when they are learning to write more complex sentences.

When I Went On The Mountain Slide

One time in Smuggler's Notch, I had my summer vacation. And one of the many adventures is when I went on the giant, twisty . . . mountain slide! And well, here's my story.

With my family, I went to the mountain slide. I went to the changing room with my mom.

"Mom," I said, "should I go on the mountain slide?"

"Sure! Only if you want to," she said.

"But I don't know if I want to or not," I said.

"Well it's up to you, you know," she said.

I thought about it for a while, then looked up at the ceiling and twirled my finger on my nose. I was nervous because I never went on a water slide before.

When I got outside, the first thing I saw was the mountain slide.

I sighed. "Hmmm, should I go on the mountain slide?" I thought.

The second thing I saw was my dad and brother. "Hi!" they said, waving. I didn't respond.

Then I said to my mom, "Mom, I'm going on."

"Congratulations," she said.

Then I went to the slide . . .

When I got to the top, I held my breath, then I let it out. The lifeguard who pushes you said to me, "Do you want to be pushed forward, backward, or twisty?"

"Twisty," I said. And I really meant it!

I got in my tube and put my feet into the water. The lifeguard asked me some questions.

As I went down the slide, the water splashed into my eyes and I covered them so they wouldn't get wet. My arms also got wet because they were sloshing around and around in the water like worms in a thunderstorm. And the water was cold on my arms.

"Wahoo!" I screamed. I went side to side, back and forth, because the water was going up on all sides of the pool. SPLASH!!!

As I got out of the water, my mom hugged me and congratulated me. "Well done."

After that I said, "Can I go again?"

"Okay, fine," she said.

I felt proud of myself. Now I can do it, I thought.

The End

Abby's personal narrative

What's Up in the Field of Grass?

When you think of grass, what comes to mind?

When asked, some people said they never even thought about it. "Green and onion, because of onion grass," said Carrie Bennet. "I also associate it with the outdoors and nature."

Nobody said anything about how important grass is, though. It's one of those things you take for granted in life. You don't really stop to think about or look at grass. Grass is used in so many ways, here are a few.

• Many animals, such as cows, eat grass and so do humans. Cows have little bugs in their stomachs to help them digest grass.

During the summer, cows chow on the green grass outside. In the colder seasons, farmers have to bring their cows hay, another type of grass.

Did you know that rice is grass? Yep, and sugar is made from a type of grass called sugarcane.

• Lots of little bugs depend upon grass as shelter. Spiders, beetles, crickets, grasshoppers and lots of other insects live among the thin, green blades. They use grass as a means of protection.

• Grass adds beauty to the world. Without grass, the world would be a desert of dark, brown dirt.

• Grass also helps prevent erosion. It keeps soil and sand tied to the ground. If we didn't have grass then when a wind picked up, woosh, there would go your front yard.

Grass is essential in more ways than one. I don't know where the world would be without it. Next time you pass a patch of grass, you should stop to think about how important it is, and be grateful that it's there.

Helaina's feature article

Assessment Notes for _____ Date _____

What am I learning about this student as a writer?	What do I need to teach this student?

(T) is the symbol for Teaching Point.   (G) is the s

14   Strategic Writing Conferences: *Teacher'sGuide*

Assessment Notes For ___Syeda___   Dates __9/5-10/5__

What am I learning about this student as a writer?	What do I need to teach this student?
9/15 topic = "My vacation in D.C." - she's writing an "all about" entry in her writers notebook, events in time order - What's her point? She "likes to be with her cousin Amanda, who is like a sister." (T) write entries about small important moments, not the whole topic 9/23 draft "Seeing Amanda in Washington D.C." - has written (mostly) about the parts of the trip connected to Amanda - is "adding detail" to her draft - wants to share her piece with "the class" (T) writing can go beyond the class into the world (to Amanda!) 9/25 observe : peer conferring with Bonnie 10/5 topic = "Getting My Brother Into Trouble" - she says she wants her piece to be about "how much I love getting my brother in trouble" - wants to share her piece with other kids with siblings - eager to jump into her draft (T) write a plan before drafting	(G) Write to get a point across about a topic (G) write about the parts of an experience that help you get your point across (G) write for audiences outside of "the class" (G) strategies for planning a draft

(T) is the symbol for teaching point.   (G) is the symbol for instructional goal.

Viewing *Carl on Camera: Modeling Strategic Writing Conferences* DVD

You can use the *Carl on Camera: Modeling Strategic Writing Conferences* DVD, which models eleven conferences, when you are learning how to do the conferences and/or when in a study group or inservice.

Use the DVD When You're Learning How to Do the Corresponding Conferences

When you are learning to do a conference that is modeled on the DVD, view the conference first to get a feel for how it looks and sounds "in action." The DVD can be an invaluable resource when you're working to add a conference to your teaching repertoire. The conferences that appear on the DVD are indicated on the conferences in the three conference books.

The eleven conferences featured on the DVD can also help you learn how to do the other conferences. By getting a feel for the pacing of these conferences, you will have a better understanding of how the other conferences go.

The Eleven Conferences Modeled on the DVD

Book 1: *Topics*

Book 2: *Drafts*

Book 3: *Finished Projects*

Use the DVD in a Conferring Study Group or Inservice

You can also view the conferences on the DVD as part of a course on the "how to's" of conferring. If you're a teacher, you could take this course yourself. If you're a literacy coach, you might lead this course with teachers you're mentoring or as part of study group or inservice.

Whether you choose self-study or decide to build a course around the eleven model conferences, you can explore the conferences either sequentially or by topic. View just the ones that meet your own specific needs—or the needs shared by the teachers you coach. To view the writing conferences by topic, refer to the list of conferences that appears at the beginning of the sections that follow.

Topic 1: What Is the Tone of a Writing Conference?

Model Conferences

▶ Brendan (Book 1: *Topics,* Conference 5, "Finding a Topic by Mining a Writing Territory")

▶ Ashley (Book 1: *Topics,* Conference 16, "Developing a Topic by Reflecting on Its Significance")

▶ Kansas (Book 2: *Drafts,* Conference 24, "Crafting a Scene by Describing Character Actions")

Writing conferences are, first and foremost, *conversations* between a teacher and a student about writing. When conferences have a conversational tone, the student feels comfortable and is more willing to share what he's doing as a writer. This information helps you identify the student's area of need and make an accurate decision about what to teach. The student is more receptive to what you teach when he feels comfortable with you in a conference.

To help you get a sense of the conversational tone of a writing conference, watch the conference with Brendan (Book 1: *Topics,* Conference 5). As you watch the conference, pay attention to the following aspects:

▶ I sit side by side with Brendan. As I talk and listen, I look at Brendan throughout the conference.

▶ I show curiosity about Brendan as a writer by asking what he is doing and asking other questions.

▶ I listen carefully to what Brendan tells me and restate what I hear.

▌ I maintain a positive tone. I point out what I think Brendan is doing well as a writer.

▌ Brendan is comfortable talking with me, right from the beginning of the conference. He is willing to tell me that he's having some trouble as a writer: He doesn't know what to write about. Brendan is visibly excited when I tell him that I'm going to teach him a strategy for finding a topic to write about.

◆ For further information about tone, view Part 2, "Conferences Are Conversations" and "Show Students That You Care" of *Carl on Camera: Introducing Strategic Writing Conferences* or read pages 6–7 of *How's It Going? A Practical Guide to Conferring with Student Writers* (Anderson, 2000).

After viewing the conference with Brendan, you can continue to explore the tone of writing conferences by viewing any of the other conferences on the DVD. You might continue with the conferences with Ashley (Book 1: *Topics,* Conference 16) or Kansas (Book 2: *Drafts,* Conference 24). As you watch the conferences, ask yourself the following questions to help you think about their tone:

▌ How does the way that Carl and the student sit together help the student feel comfortable with the conference?

▌ In what ways does Carl demonstrate curiosity about what the student is doing?

▌ In what ways does Carl listen carefully to what the student tells him?

▌ In what ways is Carl positive about what the student is doing as a writer?

▌ In what ways does the student show that he/she is comfortable with the conference?

Once you have watched one or several conferences, it's time to apply what you've learned to your own conferences. As you confer with students, try to create a conversational tone. Try some of the teaching moves you saw in the conferences, and look for signs that your students are comfortable with you. It can be helpful to have a colleague with you as you confer, to give you feedback later about the tone.

Topic 2: What Is the Goal of a Writing Conference?

Model Conferences

❱ Trevor (Book 2: *Drafts,* Conference 21, "Crafting a Scene with Precise Details: Actions, Dialogue, and Thoughts")

❱ Cooper (Book 3: *Finished Projects,* Conference 3, "Revising by Focusing an 'All About' Story")

❱ Allison (Book 3: *Finished Projects,* Conference 4, "Revising by Focusing on Important Scenes")

In a writing conference, the teacher focuses on teaching one writing strategy or craft technique, with the goal that the student will add it to his writing repertoire. You want the student to use the strategy again when he composes in the future. Don't try to "fix up" everything that could be improved in the student's writing; you are the student's teacher, not his editor.

To help you understand this important conferring concept, watch the conference with Cooper (Book 3: *Finished Projects,* Conference 3). Notice that even though Cooper has written a draft that's several pages long, she is taught just one thing: how to focus a piece of writing. I don't review Cooper's draft with her, page by page, and make a series of suggestions that would improve every aspect of it. Instead, I teach Cooper a strategy for focusing that she will hopefully use the rest of her life. (If you're wondering when I would focus on the other areas of need, the answer is in future writing conferences.) Every conference in *Carl on Camera: Modeling Strategic Writing Conferences* DVD has the same precise focus on teaching just one writing strategy or craft technique (see "The Singular Focus of Each Model Conference" table, page 47). For ex-

ample, the conference with Trevor (Book 2: *Drafts*, Conference 21) focuses on how to write precise narrative detail, and the conference with Allison (Book 3: *Finished Projects*, Conference 4) focuses on the strategy of identifying and revising one important scene. As you watch these two conferences, ask yourself:

▶ What is the one writing strategy or craft technique that Carl teaches?

▶ How can the student use the one strategy Carl teaches in future writing?

The Singular Focus of Each Model Conference

Model Conference	The One Strategy or Craft Technique Taught
Ivan Book 1: *Topics,* Conference 4	Identify and use "writing territories," topics he is passionate about.
Brendan Book 1: *Topics,* Conference 5	Find topics and create a web to discover many ways to write about a single writing territory.
Ashley Book 1: *Topics,* Conference 16	Develop a topic by reflecting on its significance.
Michael Book 2: *Drafts,* Conference 8	Make a detailed plan for a narrative piece before starting to write.
Trevor Book 2: *Drafts,* Conference 21	Write a scene with precise narrative details— actions, dialogue, and thoughts.
Kansas Book 2: *Drafts,* Conference 24	Write character actions with precision.
Cameron Book 3: *Finished Projects,* Conference 1	Revise a draft by adding details that elaborate on the topic.
Cooper Book 3: *Finished Projects,* Conference 3	Revise an "all about" story by focusing on an important scene.
Allison Book 3: *Finished Projects,* Conference 4	Identify scenes that especially convey the message, and revise these scenes first.
Haley Book 3: *Finished Projects,* Conference 17	Edit a draft for spelling and punctuation errors by reading aloud.
Dillon Book 3: *Finished Projects,* Conference 22	Know when to use the conjunction *and*—and when not to.

◆ For further information about focusing a conference on just one strategy, view Part 2, "Conferences Help Students Become Better Writers," of *Carl on Camera: Introducing Strategic Writing Conferences* DVD or read pages 7–14 of *How's It Going? A Practical Guide to Conferring with Student Writers* (Anderson, 2000).

Once you have watched one or several conferences, it's time to try out what you've learned in your own conferences. As you confer with students, focus on teaching just one writing strategy or craft technique. Resist the urge to walk through the student's writing with her, pointing out several things that she could do to improve it. After you confer, ask yourself, "What's the one thing that I taught in this conference that the student can use again and again, from now on?" It can be helpful to have a colleague with you as you confer, to give you feedback later about your success in teaching just one strategy.

Topic 3: *What Is the Structure of a Writing Conference?*

Model Conferences:

▶ Ivan (Book 1: *Topics*, Conference 4, "Finding a Topic by Brainstorming Writing Territories")

▶ Kansas (Book 2: *Drafts*, Conference 24, "Crafting a Scene by Describing Character Actions")

▶ Haley (Book 3: *Finished Projects*, Conference 17, "Editing for Clarity by Reading Aloud")

Writing conferences have two parts (see "The First Part of the Writing Conference: Identifying the Student's Needs" and "The Second Part of the Writing Conference: Teaching the Writing Strategy or Craft Technique," pages 5–7). In the first part, we identify an area of need that a student has as a writer. In the second, we teach the student a writing strategy or craft technique that addresses the area of need.

To see the two-part conference structure, watch the conference with Haley (Book 3: *Finished Projects,* Conference 17). In the first part of the conference, I find out that Haley needs to learn a more effective editing strategy to help her locate the errors in her writing. The strategy she relies on, editing by reading her draft to herself silently, is not the most effective editing strategy. Then, in the second part of the conference, I teach her one of these more effective editing strategies: reading her writing aloud for errors.

Watch the conference with Haley again. This time, look at the two parts of the conference in more detail. Notice *how* I find out Haley's area of need in the first part of the conference. I begin with an **open-ended question** that invites Haley to say what she's doing as a writer. Then I ask several **follow-up questions** to get more information about how Haley edits her writing. I **look at her writing** to gauge how effective her editing has been.

In the second part of the conference, notice *how* I teach Haley a writing strategy. I start by giving **feedback** about Haley's editing. Then I **teach** Haley the strategy of reading a draft aloud to look for errors. After I have Haley **try out** this strategy briefly, I **link** the conference to Haley's independent work. I let her know that I expect her to continue using the strategy when the conference is over, both with the draft she's working on and with future drafts.

You can continue to explore the topic of the structure of a writing conference by viewing several other conferences on *Carl on Camera: Modeling Strategic Writing Conferences* DVD. Although all the conferences follow the same two-part structure, two good ones to watch are the conference with Ivan (Book 1: *Topics,* Conference 4), in which I teach a strategy for finding a topic to write about, and the conference with Kansas (Book 2: *Drafts,* Conference 24), in which I teach how to write specific details. As you watch the conferences with their structure in mind, think about (or discuss) the following questions.

After viewing the first part of the conference:
▶ What area of need did Carl identify?
▶ What steps did Carl take to identify this area of need?
After viewing the second part of the conference:
▶ What writing strategy or craft technique did Carl teach?
▶ What steps did Carl take to teach the strategy or craft technique?

◆ For further information about the structure of a writing conference, view Part 2, "Conferences Have a Predictable Structure," and Part 3, "The Teacher's Role in a Writing Conference," of *Carl on Camera: Introduction to Strategic Writing Conferences* DVD or read pages 14–17 and 25–68 of *How's It Going? A Practical Guide to Conferring with Student Writers* (Anderson, 2000).

Topic 4: What Is Effective Teaching in a Writing Conference?

Once you have watched one or several conferences, it's time to try out what you've learned in your own conferences. As you confer with students, keep the two-part structure of the conference in mind. Try following the steps in each conference part. It can be helpful to have a colleague with you as you confer, to give you feedback later about the structure of your conference.

Model Conferences

▶ Ashley (Book 1: *Topics*, Conference 16, "Developing a Topic by Reflecting on Its Significance")

▶ Kansas (Book 2: *Drafts*, Conference 24, "Crafting a Scene by Describing Character Actions")

▶ Cameron (Book 3: *Finished Projects*, Conference 1, "Revising by Adding Text")

There are several important teaching "moves" in the **teach** step of a writing conference. They are to explain *what* you are teaching the student, *why* it's important for the student to learn the strategy or technique, and *how* to do the strategy or technique.

To see effective teaching, watch the conference with Kansas (Book 2: *Drafts*, Conference 24). I begin the **teach** part of the conference by **naming** what I'm going to teach: "to write precise actions." Then I discuss **why** it's important to learn how to write precise actions and explain **how** to write precise actions: by envisioning different kinds of body actions. I share examples from the model text *Fireflies!* by Julie Brinckloe (1985).

◆ For further information about effective teaching during a conference, view Part 3, "The Teacher's Role in a Writing Conference," of *Carl on Camera: Introduction to Strategic Writing Conferences* DVD. If you're leading a study group or inservice on conferring, you may view the DVD when you explore Topic 4.

You can continue to explore the topic of effective teaching by viewing several other conferences. Although all of conferences model the same effective teaching moves, two good ones to watch are the conference with Ashley (Book 1: *Topics,* Conference 16), in which I teach how to reflect on the meaning of topics, and the conference with Cameron (Book 3: *Finished Projects,* Conference 1), in which I teach how to revise by adding to a draft.

In some conferences, I don't explicitly explain why it's important to learn the strategy. This is because I'm teaching in response to an area of need specifically named by the student. For example, in the conference with Ivan (Book 1: *Topics,* Conference 4), Ivan complains that he's not sure what to write about. Why did I decide to teach him to brainstorm writing territories? To have topics to write about, of course.

As you watch the conferences with effective teaching in mind, think about (or discuss) the following questions:

▶ What writing strategy or craft technique did Carl name and then teach?

▶ What did Carl say to explain why it is important to learn this strategy or technique?

▶ What did Carl say in order to explain how to do the strategy or technique?

Once you have watched one or several conferences, it's time to try out what you've learned in your own conferences. As you confer with students, keep the effective teaching moves in mind. It can be helpful to have a colleague with you as you confer, to give you feedback later about how effective your teaching was.

Topic 5: How Do We Use a Model Text in a Writing Conference?

Model Conferences

❯ Ivan (Book 1: *Topics,* Conference 4, "Finding a Topic by Brainstorming Writing Territories")

❯ Kansas (Book 2: *Topics,* Conference 24, "Crafting a Scene by Describing Character Actions")

❯ Cameron (Book 3: *Drafts,* Conference 1, "Revising by Adding Text")

When you **teach** during a writing conference, it's important to use a model text to help the student "see" what the strategy or technique looks like when an experienced writer uses it. It helps the student envision using the strategy herself. Also, when you use a model text , you give the student guided practice "reading like a writer"—the habit that writers have of learning from other writers when they read their writing (see Book 3: *Finished Projects,* Conference 28, "Reading Like a Writer with a Self-Chosen Author").

You can use a published piece of writing, such as a picture book, excerpt from a memoir or novel, or an article from a magazine or newspaper, as a model text. Or you can use an example of your own writing, such as an entry from your writer's notebook or a draft you have written.

In many of the conferences in *Carl on Camera: Modeling Strategic Writing Conferences* DVD, I use a model text to teach the student, and you can watch them to see how I use the text to teach in these conferences.

To see how a model text is used, view the conference with Kansas (Book 2: *Drafts,* Conference 24). I use Julie Brinckloe's *Fireflies!,* a

Model Texts Used in Conferences

Conference	Model Text
Ivan Book 1: *Topics*, Conference 4	Entry from Carl's writer's notebook
Brendan Book 1: *Topics*, Conference 5	Entry from Carl's writer's notebook
Ashley Book 1: *Topics*, Conference 16	Entry from Carl's writer's notebook
Michael Book 2: *Drafts*, Conference 8	Carl's plan for a piece of writing
Trevor Book 2: *Drafts*, Conference 21	Excerpt from Jean Little's *Little by Little*
Kansas Book 2: *Drafts*, Conference 24	Excerpts from Julie Brinckloe's *Fireflies!*
Cameron Book 3: *Finished Projects*, Conference 1	Carl's draft "Anzia's Last First Day of School at P.S. 321" with revisions
Allison Book 3: *Finished Projects*, Conference 4	Donald Crews' *Shortcut*
Dillon Book 3: *Finished Projects*, Conference 22	Excerpt from Jean Little's *Little by Little*

well-known picture book, to teach Kansas how to write precise actions in her narratives. As you watch the conference with the use of model texts in mind, notice that:

▶ I have the book *Fireflies!* with me for the conference. When I want to use the book as a model, it is right there for me. I don't have to walk elsewhere in the classroom to search for it, wasting valuable time. (In fact, I usually carry around several of my favorite model texts when I confer.)

▶ I put *Fireflies!* right between Kansas and me so that she can easily see the text as I refer to it.

▶ To explain how to write precise actions in a narrative, I read a few short excerpts of *Fireflies!* aloud while Kansas follows along. I am very familiar with the text and locate these excerpts easily during the conference.

◆ For further information about using model texts in conferences, read pages 109–137 of *How's It Going? A Practical Guide to Conferring with Student Writers* (Anderson, 2000). If you're leading a study group or inservice on conferring, you may want to view the DVD and/or read this section of *How's It Going* when you explore Topic 5.

❱ I use the excerpts from *Fireflies!* as examples of how to write precise actions. I connect the examples to Kansas' bicycle story by having her imagine the specific actions she made in the story (what she did with her feet, hands, and face).

You can continue to explore the topic of using a model text in a conference by viewing several other conferences on *Carl on Camera: Modeling Strategic Writing Conferences* DVD. To see how other kinds of model texts are used, view the conference with Ivan (Book 1: *Topics,* Conference 4), in which I use an entry from my writer's notebook, and the conference with Cameron (Book 3: *Finished Projects,* Conference 1), in which I use a draft of my own writing—with revisions marked. As you watch the conferences with model texts in mind, think about (or discuss) the following questions:

❱ How does Carl position the text so that both he and the student can view it?

❱ How does Carl use the text to explain the writing strategy or craft technique that he is teaching?

Once you have watched one or several conferences, it's time to try using model texts in your own conferences. Since many of the conferences in *Strategic Writing Conferences* include a sample model text, you could start by using one of them. Or if you would like to use a favorite book or some of your own writing samples instead, go ahead. Whatever model texts you choose, keep in mind how the texts are positioned and referred to during your conferences. It can be helpful to have a colleague with you as you confer, to give you feedback later about how effectively you taught using the model text.

Making the Conferences in *Strategic Writing Conferences* Your Own

THE GOAL OF *Strategic Writing Conferences* isn't to give you conference scripts to memorize and then recite when you confer with students. Rather, it is to provide templates for conferences that, over time, you'll make your own. It is likely that you will make changes to the conferences, especially by using your own experiences and writing samples and by choosing your own model texts.

Use Your Own Experience and Writing

In the "Share Your Writing" section of the conferences, you'll find stories of my writing experiences, explanations of how I approach writing tasks, and samples of my writing. Although you can certainly share my experiences, explanations, and writing with your students, you can also add a "writer to writer" element by sharing your own.

Some teachers feel intimidated by the idea of sharing their writing with students. You don't have to write like author Cynthia Rylant to be a good model for your students—only Cynthia Rylant can write like Cynthia Rylant, after all! Just remember that as an adult writer, you *do* know a lot about writing, and your students will benefit immensely when you share your experiences and writing.

How will you know what to share about yourself in a conference? As you read the "Share Your Writing" section, ask yourself, "What similar experiences have I had as a writer that would make sense for me to share?" Then share them. Ask yourself, "How do I do this as a writer?" Then share the way you do it. Imagine ways of sharing your own writing with students. You may already have a writer's notebook and drafts of pieces that you could substitute for my writing samples in a conference. If not, then try the writing strategy or craft technique described in the conference—and then share your writing with students.

Choose Your Own Model Texts

Another way to personalize the conferences is by substituting other pieces of literature for the ones suggested in the "Share Model Texts" section. The suggested texts are some of my personal favorites and have been field-tested by me and many other writing teachers, in many classrooms, but there are good reasons to use others.

The first is that you or your students must care deeply about the text. Model texts are powerful exemplars of good writing for students because the texts have moved them in some way—for example, making them laugh, cry, or want to take action in the world. Students are curious about how the authors created this response in them. If you or your students have a ho-hum response to a text (read the text to the class to introduce it before you use it in conferences), then try a different one.

It's quite possible that your students have encountered one of the model texts in a previous grade. Although it's always possible to learn more from studying a text more closely, substituting a different text can energize students.

If a model text is too advanced for a student, try a more appropriate one. After all, if a student has trouble comprehending the text, then he will have difficulty understanding why the writer used a particular craft to get across the meaning.

How do you find substitutes for the model texts in *Strategic Writing Conferences*? Here's the good news: Finding models of genres that students typically write in today has never been easier. Appendix C lists numerous resources.

Once you've located texts, read them to see which ones contain the crafts you want to teach. For example, to find a different text to use in a conference on teaching how to write "defining details" (Book 2: *Drafts*, Conference 25), read several narrative texts, looking for examples of well-written details.

In addition to sharing your own writing and experience and using different model texts, you will make the conferences "your own" by using your own words to teach—especially after you have held a particular conference again and again. The goal of *Strategic Writing Conferences* isn't to create clones of Carl Anderson; rather, it's to offer scaffolding so that you find your own individual way of teaching the things that students need to learn to be effective, powerful writers.

Assessing Students' Growth as Writers

How will you know if the hard work of using *Strategic Writing Conferences* is paying off for you and, most importantly, for your students? You should see some immediate results when you have successful conferences. Check in with each student five or ten minutes after you confer in order to "hear" the thinking and see the writing the student does in response. You should see evidence that the student tried out the writing strategy or craft technique that you taught. Keep in mind that it would be unfair to expect the student to use the strategy flawlessly, especially if you just taught it for the first time. Proficiency with a strategy comes with practice over time, in many pieces of writing, and with more support for it in future conferences. (If the student doesn't follow through with a strategy, it could be that she didn't understand your expectation that she would try the strategy in her draft. Or perhaps she didn't understand the strategy; you may need to confer again and try a new approach to teaching the concept.)

Over the school year, you will find that students add the writing strategies and craft techniques to their writing repertoire or "toolkit." This is most likely to happen if you don't try to teach a different lesson each time you confer with a student. It's best to identify a few areas of need as priorities—and confer only about those areas, several times each, over several months or even the whole year. That means that you may have to revisit the same teaching point again with a student, fine-tuning it each time to respond to what the student has internalized. Then the student will learn to use it well.

Look for evidence that a student is internalizing a writing strategy or craft technique that you've taught. During a conference, a student may tell you that he's using a strategy or technique you've taught in a previous conference. It may be that the student is using it well enough that you don't need to revisit it. Or you might decide that the student *does* need to learn more about the strategy, so you focus on it again.

You'll see a second kind of evidence in students' writing. If your conferences are effective, you will see that students are using the writing strategies or craft techniques in their writer's notebook and when they compose new drafts—weeks and months after the conferences. You'll notice this while you're conferring with a student, while you are skimming a draft, when your class is having a writing celebration and you read the finished pieces, and when you're evaluating finished pieces at the end of a unit of study.

When you see a student using writing strategies and craft techniques that you've taught in conferences, point it out! If you see a student use a strategy while you're conferring with him, compliment him orally on the spot. If you see a student use a strategy while you're reading her writing during a writing celebration or after a unit of study, give brief written feedback. Some teachers even include an item on their assessment rubrics that gives students feedback for continuing to use strategies or techniques that they learned in previous conferences.

It's in these moments—when you can give students kudos for continuing to use what you've taught with increasing proficiency—that you'll feel a well-earned sense of pride in students. And in yourself, too, for what you have accomplished: You have learned how to confer powerfully. The challenging work of learning to do the conferences in *Strategic Writing Conferences* has indeed paid off—for you and your students.

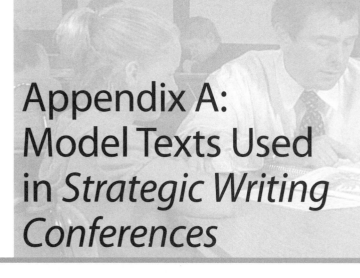

Appendix A: Model Texts Used in *Strategic Writing Conferences*

Brinckloe, Julie. 1985. *Fireflies!* New York: Simon & Schuster Children's Publishing Division.

Butler, Dori Hillestad. 1995. "New Kid." *Cricket* 22 (12).

Condor, Bob. 1994. "Operating with Spare Parts: Peek at Your Body's 'Extra' Pieces." *Chicago Tribune: Kid News* 1 (May 3).

Crews, Donald. 1996. *Shortcut.* New York: HarperTrophy.

Downey, Charles. 1998. "The Grossest Things You Can Think of May One Day Save Your Life." *Boy's Life* (December).

Fletcher, Ralph. 2005. *Marshfield Dreams: When I Was a Kid.* New York: Henry Holt and Company.

Hesse, Karen. 1999. *Come on, Rain!* New York: Scholastic.

Larrick, Nancy anad Wendy Lamb. 1991. *To Ride a Butterfly: Original Pictures, Stories, Poems, & Songs for Children.* New York: Bantam Doubleday Dell.

Lawler, Janet. 2005. "Cami's First Soccer Game." *Highlights for Children* 60 (7).

Little, Jean. 1987. *Little by Little.* New York: Penguin Books.

Long, D.S. 1990. "Cat Talk." Originally published in *School Journal* 3 (1). Reprinted in *Cricket* 21 (2).

Macaulay, Ellen. 1998. "The Rattler Tattler." *Boys' Quest* 3 (5).

MacLachlan, Patricia. 1991. *Journey.* New York: Bantam Doubleday Dell Books for Young Readers.

Meds Maps, Inc. *Cape Cod Guide.* Meds Maps, Inc.: Harwich, MA.

Musselman, Kelly. 2004. "Clean Up Your Act." *Highlights for Children.*

Myers, Jack. 2006. "How Does My Glow-in-the-Dark Stuff Glow?" *Highlights for Children: Science Letters* (November).

Polacco, Patricia. 1994. *My Rotten Redheaded Older Brother.* New York: Simon & Schuster Children's Publishing Division.

Polacco, Patricia. 1999. *My Ol' Man.* New York: Penguin Putnam Books for Young Readers.

Purdom, Candace. 1994. "Peer Pressure: Afraid You'll Cave?" *Chicago Tribune: Kid News* 5 (August 23).

Purdom, Candace. 1994. "So a Big, Bad Bully Is Coming after You . . ." *Chicago Tribune: Kid News* 1 (August 23).

Reifsnyder, Cheryl. 2006. "Quick-Thinking Meerkats." *Highlights for Children* 61 (9).

Rylant, Cynthia. 1993. *The Relatives Came.* New York: Simon & Schuster Children's Publishing Division.

Sendak, Maurice. 1988. *Where the Wild Things Are.* New York: HarperTrophy.

Soto, Gary. 2000. "The Marble Champ." In *Baseball in April and Other Stories.* Orlando, FL: Harcourt Children's Books.

TIME For Kids. 1999. "Hooked!" *TIME For Kids* 4 (March 12).

Yolen, Jane. 1987. *Owl Moon.* New York: Penguin Putnam Books for Young Readers.

Appendix B: Model Texts from Children's Magazines and Newspapers

The model texts from children's magazines and newspapers follow this reference list. They are printed in full for use as reproducibles in your classroom.

- "New Kid" by Dori Butler

- "Operating with Spare Parts: Peek at Your Body's 'Extra' Pieces" by Bob Condor

- "The Grossest Things You Can Think of May One Day Save Your Life" by Charles Downey

- "Cami's First Soccer Game" by Janet Lawler

- "Cat Talk" by Don S. Long

- "The Rattler Tattler" by Ellen Macaulay

- "Clean Up Your Act" by Kelly Musselman

- "How Does My 'Glow-in-the-Dark' Stuff Glow?" by Dr. Jack Myers

- "Peer Pressure: Afraid You'll Cave?" by Candace Purdom

- "So a Big, Bad Bully Is Coming After You . . ." by Candace Purdom

- "Quick-Thinking Meerkats" by Cheryl Reifsnyder

- "Hooked!" from *TIME For Kids*

New Kid

Kayla hated being the new kid. She hated being stared at. The boy who sat across from her had been staring at her since she sat down.

Kayla was about to tell him to take a picture, it lasts longer, when suddenly he said, "Nice shirt."

Kayla glanced at her AAU Junior Olympics shirt.

"I've got one just like it at home," the boy said.

"You were at the Junior Olympics?" Kayla asked. What were the odds of her running into another Junior Olympics competitor at her new school?

"Yup. Basketball," he said proudly. "What's your sport?"

"Table tennis," Kayla replied.

"Oh." He rolled his eyes.

Kayla had seen that reaction before. She crossed her arms. "I suppose you think table tennis isn't a real sport," she said.

"Well, you have to admit Ping-Pong just isn't as physical as basketball." Kayla cringed when he said Ping-Pong. "It's a rec room game," he went on. "Like pool. Or checkers."

Kayla wanted to wipe the smirk off this kid's face. "Maybe you and I should play a match sometime," she said.

He smiled as though this was the most ridiculous thing he'd ever heard. "You're challenging me?" he asked. He turned to the boy who sat behind him. That boy raised his eyebrows as if Kayla had to be an idiot for challenging the other boy to anything.

Kayla ignored him. "Are you up to a challenge?" she asked the first boy.

"Name the time and place," he said.

"My house. After school today," Kayla said.

"You got it," he said.

Later Kayla found out the boy's name was Michael Savitch. She also found out Michael didn't just play basketball. He played practically everything.

"Do you really think you can beat him?" a short girl with glasses asked Kayla. Her name was Holly.

"Maybe," Kayla said.

"Could we watch?" asked Holly's friend Mindy.

"Sure," Kayla said.

Holly and Mindy invited Kayla to eat lunch with then. They introduced her to Jessica. Jessica introduced her to Paula. Paula introduced her to Sara.

And each time, Kayla was introduced as "the girl who's going to beat Michael Savitch at table tennis."

"Wow!" Each girl looked at Kayla with admiration.

Was Michael really that good? Kayla wondered. What if she made a fool of herself? What if Michael actually beat her? Would Holly, Mindy, Jessica, Paula, and Sara still want to be her friends?

Kayla's mom looked surprised when Kayla came home with nine people that day. "We're going to play some table tennis," Kayla said.

Kayla grabbed a bag of apples from the fridge and headed down to the basement. The other kids clattered down the stairs behind her.

"We'll have to move some boxes," Kayla said. "We're not quite moved in yet."

"No problem," Michael said. He and the boys picked up boxes at one end of the table and set them around the corner. Kayla and the girls moved the boxes from the other end of the table.

The boys stopped when they had cleared a six-foot area behind the table. "You need to clear all the way to the wall," Kayla said.

"What for?" one of the boys asked. "Are we here for Ping-Pong or cheap labor?"

"Table tennis," Kayla said through gritted teeth. "And I need lots of room to play."

"OOOOO," said the boys. But they grudgingly moved the rest of the boxes. Kayla crawled under the table and opened the box labeled table tennis supplies.

When everything was set up, Michael asked, "Could we warm up a little?"

"Sure," Kayla said.

The girls lined up along one side of the table. The boys lined up along the other. The only sound in the room was the plink plunk of the ball as it bounced from court to court.

If Michael had any tricks, he didn't show them during their easy volleys. Kayla didn't show hers either.

"You ready to play?" Kayla asked.

Michael nodded. He won the serve, and the game began. Michael wasn't bad. Kayla was better.

Michael's main problem was not knowing when to go for the kill shot. He also got confused when Kayla gave him a loop shot.

Kayla had Michael running all over his court. The kids who were watching the game had to move away from the table so they wouldn't get plowed over. Kayla won the first game 21 to 7. The girls cheered and the boys groaned.

"That's O.K.," Michael panted. His damp hair was plastered to his forehead. "I'm warmed up now."

Sure you are, Kayla thought to herself. She hadn't even shown him her sidespin yet.

The second game was over even faster than the first. Kayla won that one 21 to 5. The girls jumped up and down, clapping. "She won!" Holly cried. "She beat Michael Savitch!" Mindy yelled.

Kayla bounced the ball on the table a few times and looked over at Michael. "Still think table tennis isn't a physical game?" she asked.

Michael wiped his face with the bottom of his shirt. He didn't say anything.

"Should we try another nonphysical game?" Kayla asked. "Maybe eightball?"

Michael eyed the pool table wearily. "Give me a few days to practice up first," he said.

Kayla smiled. She'd made her point. Good thing, too. She was awful at pool.

—Dori Butler

Operating with Spare Parts: Peek at Your Body's "Extra" Pieces

Lie back, close your eyes—and imagine that your doc has just removed your appendix. Before you holler, "Hey, put that back!" don't panic. You can do without it.

Didn't know your body had a spare part? Wait, there are more. Let's take a peek:

The best example is that appendix. Most doctors say we can do just fine, thank you, without it.

Dr. Robert J. Touloukin of Yale University says it's been thousands of years, probably, since the appendix was considered a working part of the body. About the size of your little finger and attached to the large intestine at the right side of your lower stomach, it used to help digest food; now it pretty much lies around and does nothing. Occasionally, the appendix does get in the act—but only as a troublemaker when it swells from infection. If that's going to happen, it usually does in kids ages 5–12. Doctors often will remove the appendix before it becomes too enlarged.

You can also get along just fine without tonsils, that pair of stubby glands at the back of your throat. Tonsils aren't good-for-nothings like the appendix; they help fight off germs. But tonsils can also become enlarged from serious infection (your basic mega-major-league sore throat). This usually happens at least once to kids up to age 7, when tonsils grow to their biggest size before shrinking.

Twenty years ago, that one infection might have persuaded your doctor to yank your tonsils. Now, doctors will look for repeated infections before taking them out.

On the other hand, dentists won't take too long to decide on removing another spare body part, called a wisdom tooth, if it is hurting you. We all have the potential for growth in four "third molars" at the back of our mouths, top and bottom, right and left. Wisdom teeth are the most likely to be a real pain in your late teens or early 20s, but some lucky dogs among us never have any problems.

Any more parts we can spare? Well, there are *parts* of parts that can go, says Dr. Touloukin.

"We can now safely take out [diseased] sections of a lung, liver, spleen or intestine," he says, "and also one of your kidneys if the situation requires it. Kids have an incredible ability to 'remodel' these body parts."

—Bob Condor

The Grossest Things You Can Think of May One Day Save Your Life

Feeling a little under the weather? Some frog skin or pond scum might be just what you need.

Gross? Sure! Disgusting? Absolutely. Will it work? Scientists hope so.

Creepy crawly creatures have survived for millions of years without doctors. Researchers believe the compounds in their bodies that act as natural medicines could also help sick humans.

"Scientists are finding that good things can come from lowly places," says Dr. Mark S. Lacey, a specialist in spider biology.

Spider-Web Bandage

Folks living a hundred years ago had an odd remedy for cuts and scrapes: Coat them with cobwebs. Now scientists like Dr. Lacey say that remedy may not have been so odd.

Spiders aren't exactly picky eaters. They'll munch on just about anything that gets stuck in their web, no matter where the insect has been. So it makes sense that the sticky silk contains a germ-killer.

Scientists are working on turning that arachno-medicine into people medicine. "Now that we have such powerful research tools," Dr. Lacey says, "we can learn how spiders have used these chemicals."

Warts and All

Frogs are funny. Not only do they make weird noises and spring to heights that Michael Jordan would be proud of (for their size), they also live in the dirtiest, murkiest places on the planet. Yet they never get infections.

Dr. Michael Zasloff wondered why. He discovered the skin of some frogs contains a powerful antibiotic that kills germs.

With the frog skin, Dr. Zasloff developed a cream to help cure infected diabetic foot ulcers. The medicine should be released next fall.

What's That Smell?

Many times when people eat like a pig, they start to look like, well, a pig. To keep that from happening, scientists have enlisted the help of—that's right—a pig.

And they've found that help in the grossest of places: the pigs' sewage lagoon. Amid all the slime and goo and stench, scientists discovered a rare bacteria that may prevent dangerous weight gain and other fat-related problems.

The swine bacteria changes vein-clogging cholesterol—caused by ingesting too many french fries, potato chips and other greasy food—into a harmless substance that passes out of the body. Researchers say soon you might be able to swallow a pill that will flush the cholesterol right out of you.

—Charles Downey

Cami's First Soccer Game

Cami's knees wobbled as she ran onto the field.

"OK!" called Coach Wood. "Remember three things. One, use your feet, not your hands. Two, aim for the goal. Three, which way are we going, Dynamites?"

Cami pointed. She tried yelling "That way!" with her teammates, but only a squeak came out. It was her first soccer game ever. Cami had been more excited about it than starting first grade. She had even tried to wear her soccer shoes to bed last night. But now she was scared. There were too many kids, too many parents, and too many rules.

Twe-eet! The game was on! Mothers and fathers cheered. Both teams swirled around the soccer ball like a school of fish after one bit of bait. Cami ran, too, but not very close to the others.

Her best friend, Rosa, kicked the ball. It popped out beside Cami. She froze. The group headed her way, then flowed past on either side.

Mom yelled, "Run, Cami!"

Dad shouted, "Move, Cami!"

But Cami just stood there, facing her goal.

At last the whistle blew for halftime. Everyone took a short rest.

"Let's go, Cami!" Rosa yelled, pulling her back onto the field. The Dynamites faced the other way for the second half.

"Cami, you play defense," Coach said. "Try to stop the ball from getting by you, OK?"

Cami nodded and looked behind her at Joshua, the Dynamite goalie. He clapped his gloves and grinned. Cami was too nervous to smile back.

"Which way are we going, Dynamites?" Coach asked. This time Cami joined in. "That way!"

Twe-eet! Again, the players ran back and forth, up and down. But Cami still didn't budge.

Dad bellowed, "Go, Cami!"

Mom cried, "Come on, Cami!"

Cami swallowed hard. Her feet felt as if they were buried deep in beach sand. The players pounded toward her.

Who had the ball? Then she saw Rosa out in front, dribbling.

But something was not right. Cami frowned. What was it? Rosa was going the wrong way!

Cami called out, "Rosa, turn around!"

"Oh!" Rosa cried. She stopped short and tapped the ball to Cami. The player behind Rosa tripped. Several players fell on top of him, like a row of dominoes going down one by one.

"Pass it back!" Rosa urged, circling around before the team untangled.

Cami squeezed her eyes shut for just a moment. Then she kicked the ball hard to Rosa. Rosa trapped it and turned around. She dribbled all the way back and shot it into the goal. The Dynamites had scored! The referee blew the whistle.

Soon the game was over. Cami let out a deep breath. At the side of the field, her team was jumping up and down.

Rosa gave her a bear hug. "Thanks for turning me around. I was mixed up!"

Cami beamed. "You're welcome!"

Joshua tried to lift Cami off the ground. Another teammate slapped her on the back. Coach Wood led a cheer for the other team.

Cami smiled back and took a sip from her water bottle. She couldn't wait for next week's game.

—Janet Lawler

Cat Talk

Anyone can learn cat "talk." It just takes lots of practice. Cats do use sounds—you hear them when they're fighting—but cats mainly use their own special signs.

What follows is a kind of dictionary: a dictionary of Cat. Although this dictionary isn't complete, it'll get you started. Good luck!

Purring

Most people think that cats purr when they're happy. But sick and injured cats purr, too. Purring expresses friendship. Purring can also mean "dinner's served." Try it the next time you feed a cat.

Saying hello

Does your cat roll over when you come home and twitch the tip of his tail? Some people think that means "scratch my tummy." But most cats don't like their tummies touched. Rolling over is a sleepy way of saying hello.

Scent sharing

Cats have a special way of saying "you are part of my family." They rub against us with the sides of their mouth, temple, and tail. Then they sit down and lick themselves. When your cat does this to you, it is marking you with its scent. Afterward it licks its own fur to taste your scent. So if you don't want to belong to cat, move away.

You're the boss

Making yourself as flat as possible, not looking at anyone directly and keeping quiet is a way to submit in Cat. It's similar to how some people behave on their first day at a new school.

Head bumping

When cats just want to say a quick hi, they bump heads. If you have a cat among your friends, you might like to try this; it will know exactly what you mean. This is not the same as repeated bumping. That means "please, please, please."

Whisker "words"

A curious cat sticks its whiskers straight out; they twitch with excitement. Bored cats have droopy whiskers. Contented cats let their whiskers lie flat against their faces and half close their eyes. But watch out, because wide-eyed cats with flattened whiskers are frightened.

Sitting down

Sometimes we "say" things to cats we don't really mean to say. Does your cat climb on your lap when you sit down? Does it then begin to knead you with its paws, loudly purring? When mother cats lay down, this is how kittens get milk to come. By sitting down, you have, in cat language, offered to give milk!

Tail waving

One reason cats have trouble understanding us is because we don't have tails. Cats wave their tails when they're trying to make up their minds. As soon as they make a choice, the waving stops. When a cat stalks a bird, it often waves its tail. This is because it's trying to decide whether to pounce or creep.

Tail swishing

A swishing tail says something quite different. Most people learn the hard way that this means "I'm angry. Watch out."

Fluffy tail

Frightened cats "say" fluffy tail. They probably can't help themselves. It's a bit like us saying "ouch."

Flagpole tail

Some cats use a straight raised tail to say hello. Petting (sharing your scent) is a polite reply.

Teaching humans to hunt

Kittens are taught how to hunt. First they are shown how to eat mice. Next they are given dead mice to play with. Then they are given wounded mice to kill. If your cat brings a mouse home, it thinks you are old enough to learn how to hunt. Your cat will tell you what level it thinks you're up to.

Fighting talk

When two cats come together for a fight, they make themselves look big. Their fur fluffs up and they "walk tall." They stare at each other and twist their heads from side to side, as if in the middle of a bite. They show the backs of their ears and howl, hiss and spit.

If you stare at a strange cat and slowly approach, it won't like it. Staring at something calls it "prey." If your cat walks onto a book you're reading, it may have come to see what you plan to catch. Try staring at a distant chair if you want to get rid of your cat for a bit. (This is to tell a lie in Cat.)

Crab walking

Sometimes cats "say" two different things at once. When a cat is thinking about attacking and running away, it may do both. Crab walking—moving sideways—results when the front paws are retreating and the back paws are attacking.

Paw wiping

To tell a cat to get lost, try standing with your side to it and wiping the bottom of your foot against the ground. It's a very strong thing to "say," so don't do it unless you really mean it.

Claws in, claws out

A clawless pat means "I want something." If the claws are out, that's fighting talk.

Ear talk

Ears are a problem when you want to talk Cat. If you could show the backs of your ears, you could say "I'm ready to fight." Flattening your ears would say "I'm ready to protect myself." Pricked ears could show you were alert. A curious cat will say "Well, well, well, what have we here?" by approaching carefully, with ears pricked forward and twitching one at a time.

Licking

Does your cat lick you? Your cat is trying to groom you by licking your fur. You're expected to lick back. It's just another way of saying "we are a family." You can reply by stroking your cat or giving it a brush. Refusing to lick or stroke back says "I'm displeased with you."

One final hint

When cats talk, they "speak" with their tails, fur, posture, ears, eyes, and whiskers all at once. They may even make sounds. Although this dictionary separates these things, to really talk Cat you'll need to try combining them. But don't worry. A cat that loves you will understand, even when you only say one thing at a time.

—D.S. Long

The Rattler Tattler

Rattlesnakes are the Bart Simpsons of the animal world. With their menacing fangs, they're a hot choice for tattoos and biker jackets. But rattlers are more in danger than dangerous. They get no mercy! Often, people simply kill them on sight. All this for a creature that goes out of its way to avoid you and even sounds a warning if you're too close.

Since they don't stick around long enough to give you the lowdown, we'll tell you more about these slick, slithery guys.

Rattlers are solitary critters. They spend most of their day hiding from the hot sun and their enemies: foxes, kingsnakes, people with sticks. They search for food at night.

Rattlers' digestive systems operate opposite of the way ours do. We swallow our food, and it then digests in our stomach. Rattlesnakes digest food first and then swallow. Here's how: The rattler tracks its prey by smelling with its tongue (yes, you read right). It strikes its prey (let's say it's a stinky rat) and bites, releasing a powerful venom.

The rat's fading heartbeat circulates digestive enzymes from the snake that essentially break down the rat's innards: muscles, tissue, bones, the works. The rattler can then say "ahhhh" and swallow the squishy rat whole. In this way, rattlesnakes can swallow whole foods way larger than they are. It would be like you saying, "a 250-pounder with cheese, please"—then chowing down on a massive burger and not getting a gut ache!

Rattlesnake bites hurt like crazy. You swell up and turn a lovely shade of deep purple. But don't worry, there's an antidote.

So remember, the rattlesnake is a lot like the Grand Canyon. If you just stand back, you can see the beauty—but up close, things could get a little rocky.

—Ellen Macaulay

Clean Up Your Act
Splish, Splash—Time for Your Yearly Bath!

Have you ever tried to get out of taking your bath? Kids in the 18th century skipped theirs all the time—and so did their parents!

Back then, everyone thought it was unhealthy for people to take a bath. They believed bathing removed important oils from the skin, oils that protected people from disease. Most people bathed once or twice a year. If you took a bath more often than that, your neighbors thought you were weird!

People weren't too keen on changing or washing their clothes, either. They wore perfume or flowers to cover up the odor that resulted. Wealthy people's clothes were a little cleaner—but only because they could afford more outfits to change into.

The faces of both men and women were caked with makeup to cover dirt and blemishes. Black "beauty patches"—in the shapes of stars, moons, and hearts—were stuck on the face to cover up zits or scars from diseases such as smallpox.

Hair wasn't often washed or even brushed. Men wore wigs, while women sported huge, elaborate hairstyles for weeks at a time. Both were home to itchy fleas and lice.

Luckily, by the 19th century, ideas about bathing and cleanliness changed. People began to bathe weekly, usually on Saturday so they would be clean for church.

Now most people bathe and change their clothes every day. And your neighbors think that you're weird if you don't!

—Kelly Musselman

How Does My "Glow-in-the-Dark" Stuff Glow?

Glow-in-the-dark stickers and toys are made with chemicals that take up light particles, or *photons*. Scientists say these special molecules become "excited" because they are holding extra energy from the photons. Later, the molecules lose their "excitement" by giving off photons. Then they are giving off light and glowing.

—Dr. Jack Myers

Peer Pressure: Afraid You'll Cave?

You can get out of tight spots when your pals put the squeeze on

You can't see it, smell it or touch it. But it pushes you toward the same movies, clothes and music as your pals, nudges you away from your parents and closer to your friends, and has the power to bring you better grades or mega problems. At school, it's as real as the lockers in the hall and that mystery meat in the lunch line.

Is it some awesome force surrounding you? Yeah, in a way. It's a big, invisible power called peer pressure. Basically, it's that powerful feeling you have of wanting to fit in with your friends. To start off the school year, a psychologist and our kid experts help you learn more about it, so you can handle it (instead of it handling you).

What is it?

Each member in a group of friends has influence on the others. That pressure builds its own energy, almost like a tornado. Says James Gioia, a Wheaton psychologist who works with kids and families, "Instead of children being able to make decisions on their own, they are swayed by that energy and affected by what their friends think of them."

In other words, says 13-year-old Katy G., of Rockford, "You don't want to look like a dork."

Happy, happy, joy, joy

Gioia says peer pressure can be a "very positive psychological influence." In plain English, that means friends share good times, learn to socialize and work toward a goal, and great things can happen—like when a shy kid blossoms or a kid learns better study habits doing homework with friends.

Besides, Gioia says, leaning toward friends is a normal part of growing up and becoming a person separate from your parents.

Danger signs

But there's a down side to peer pressure too. "The group may not always be on solid ground," says Gioia, who adds that kids in a group may do things members would never do alone (like vandalism). "To say no and make a statement that's apart from that group puts kids on the spot."

Whether the choice is to spend all your money on the latest Nikes like your pal's, to tease someone your friends don't like, or worse, it's sometimes tough to back away. "But if kids are doing something that you feel is wrong, they're the ones with the problem," Katy says. "Some kids don't know how to act right and get friends, so they think, 'If this is the way I get friends, then I'll have to do it.'"

What you can do

Before you're swept away, try these tips to tame that tornado:

1. Know your limits. Brian T., 13, of Elmhurst, ranks things as stupid or really stupid, and knows where he draws the line. "Stupid would be like wearing a disgusting T-shirt. I'll do that because my friends would think that was cool," Brian says. "But really stupid? Like I wouldn't go out and get drunk."

2. Recognize when you're being pushed too far. "My friends have some influence on me," Katy says, "but real friends shouldn't take advantage of you. They won't force you to do stuff."

3. Make an excuse, suggest something else to do or follow Brian's advice and act dumb when you run into a sticky situation. "I just kind of walk away like I don't know what's going on," he says. "I don't care, and it's not that hard."

4. Pay attention when something feels wrong inside. "Just say this is something that I don't want to do and I won't allow myself to do," Gioia says. If your insides are confused, don't be afraid to talk to a parent or another trusted adult.

5. Make a decision and show you mean it. "Peer pressure can be very fragile and it looks toward leadership and kids who can take a stand," Gioia says. "A lot of these kids respect the statements of the strong person."

—by Candace Purdom

So a Big, Bad Bully Is Coming after You . . .

Bigger than Shaquille. Meaner than the Wicked Witch of the West. Scarier than a raptor. We're talking about the school bully.

"Bullies are angry little kids," says psychologist Alan Hirsch of the Chicago area's Capable Kid Counseling Centers. "We've worked with kids who are proud that they're bullying other children."

Often they feel bad about themselves, so bullies take it out on others. Yeah, we know, it's hard to feel sorry for someone who makes your life miserable. Here are tips on making a tough spot easier.

- Don't let the bully think it's OK to pick on you. Say how you feel. If it's too scary to face the bully, find a go-between. An adult can help, too. Sometimes a stupid rumor can build up and BAM—you've got someone all over you. Talking can resolve that.

- Being a bully's target leaves you down and lonely. New pals can bring fun times and you'll feel better about yourself. Follow your interests by signing up for outside programs and we bet you'll find kids who share things you like.

In some schools, kids get the job of hearing both sides of a problem as conflict managers. They help kids find a solution, or pass the problem on to the teacher if it's more serious. Your school can get special training info from the Community Board Program in California, 415–552–1250, or you could create your own system in your classroom.

- Ask your teacher to hold a class meeting. "A lot of kids think they are the only ones being affected," says Steve Klein, who runs the conflict management program in the Elgin schools. "But if everybody talks about it, you're probably better off."

- Find a Circle of Friends. Teachers may know about this cool technique that links a kid who is bullied with other kids who act as coaches (with tips like drop the geeky backpack, and stop raving about Barney). They watch out for the kid, too. Even if your teacher doesn't know about it, you and your friends who know what it's like to be picked on (and probably that includes everyone!) could form your own group to befriend the kid who's being tormented by a bully.

Ryan S., 10, of Hanover Park, says a Circle of Friends worked magic for a classmate who had been picked on. They ate lunch with the boy, included him in activities and told him to chill when other kids teased him. "I felt sorry for him because it's not right when someone's different, that they should be made fun of," Ryan said. "But after a while, people wanted to play with him and they treated him like one of us."

- Act fast if you are in real danger. Sometimes adults tell kids to ignore troublemakers—and some adults tell kids to fight back. But these days, bullies can be far scarier than the kid who waited to beat up your dad at recess—today's bullies could have a weapon. If you find yourself in a situation that seems scary and dangerous, go to an adult you trust right away.

—Candace Purdom

Quick-Thinking Meerkats

Dr. Marta Manser crouches in the dry grass, watching a cat-sized meerkat sniff for its breakfast. Suddenly, a high-pitched alarm call breaks the morning quiet: Hawk! The meerkat bounds toward a hiding hole, reaching it in seconds.

Dr. Manser traveled from the University of Zurich in Switzerland to South Africa's Kalahari Desert to study how meerkats find their hiding places—and to learn about how animals think. Many animals show intelligence, from toolmaking to navigating long distances. Scientists want to understand how these animals solve tricky problems.

"Meerkats are a great subject to study," Dr. Manser says. "The size of the meerkats and their small home range allow us to follow them easily on foot over the whole day."

The researchers couldn't always observe meerkats so closely. But over time, the animals got used to having people nearby. "It took a year," Dr. Manser says. "Wild meerkats typically run away when they see a person at a distance of a few hundred meters."

Avoiding Danger

A meerkat is not a cat. It's related to the mongoose. A meerkat's life depends on its ability to find shelter quickly. This animal spends five to eight hours daily searching for food such as insects, snakes, scorpions, and small mammals. During those hours, the meerkat can be attacked by hawks, jackals, or other predators. Meerkats live in groups and take turns acting as guards, standing on hind legs and watching for danger.

Dr. Manser wondered how meerkats find those botholes. Do the animals make decisions based on what they see at the moment or on what they saw in the past few minutes? Or do meerkats remember where to find their holes? Only some clever experiments would lead to answers.

Do They Backtrack?

Once researchers could follow within a few feet of the meerkats, they began to watch what meerkats did when they heard an alarm call. The research team's first question was, Do meerkats backtrack to the last hole they passed?

The team found that the meerkats almost always ran to the nearest bolthole, just as you might run to the closest bathroom in your school instead of going back to the last one you passed.

The scientists had discovered that meerkats go to the best hiding spot, even if they haven't passed it recently. But how do they find it?

Sight or Memory?

Dr. Manser's next question was, Do meerkats find the closest hole by looking for it?

The research team dug new boltholes. When a meerkat came near, the researchers played a recording of an alarm bark to make the meerkat run for shelter. If meerkats find boltholes by looking for them, they should have run to the new, easy-to-see holes. But the meerkats ignored the new holes.

The research team had answered another question. Meerkats don't find boltholes by looking for them. In fact, they run to other boltholes, even if the a hole is closer.

If meerkats don't look around and don't backtrack to find boltholes, Dr. Manser wondered, do meerkats remember where the holes are, similar to the way you remember where the bathrooms are in your school?

To test this idea, the research team covered some holes with car mats and sand. When a meerkat approached, they played the recorded alarm back and watched. The meerkats remembered where to find their holes.

"The meerkats, running over the covered boltholes, stopped at the supposed entrance," Dr. Manser says. "Some of them immediately ran to the next bolthole, while others began to dig the sand out." One meerkat dug out so much sand searching for the lost hole that the mat fell in.

Now the team had yet another answer. Even though meerkats have several thousand boltholes, they remembered exactly where the holes are.

What Are They Thinking?

Meerkats remember where to find their holes—but how? Maybe they follow specific routes in their search for food, allowing them to memorize a few "snapshots" of the landscape that they can recognize later. Or maybe their thinking is more human-like. Maybe they make a mental map of their foraging area.

Only one more study will tell. Dr. Manser doesn't mind. She loves studying meerkats.

"Some of the best moments are the early hours at their sleeping burrow when the sun rises," she says. "One after the other emerges from the burrow, some still totally sleepy while others are already fully active, just as people differ in this way."

Soon, she'll be back at one of those burrows, ready to figure out more about how meerkats think.

Mere Facts on Meerkats
Newborn Meerkats
- are born in litters of 2 to 5
- weigh about an ounce
- open their eyes when they are 10 to 14 days old

Adult Meerkats
- weigh 1½ to 2 pounds
- are 10 to 14 inches long (plus a 7- to 10-inch tail)

—Cheryl Reifsnyder

Hooked!

Some kids can't get enough of video games. Is your playing out of control?

It's 10 o'clock on a Saturday morning. David Picone, 10, and brother Ricky, 11, are soaked with sweat. There are only two seconds left in the game, and David's up by 1 point. Ricky inbounds the ball. A no-look pass, and a slamming two-handed dunk wins the game! "He shoots; he scores!" screams Ricky. "Game over. You lose!" Ricky runs around with his hands in the air. David wipes the sweat from his eyes and punches his brother in the arm.

An intense morning basketball game? Sort of. Except Ricky and David are in their basement and still in their pajamas. They are playing March Madness '98 on their Sony PlayStation. Their parents have been calling them to come upstairs for breakfast for 25 minutes. Mom and Dad are not too happy.

Video-Game Invasion

Does this scene sound familiar? No wonder. Video games have invaded the lives of American kids, and in some cases they've taken over!

More than 181 million video and computer games were sold in the U.S. last year. That's almost two games for every household! Americans spent $5.5 billion on video and computer games in 1998—25% more than in 1997. Of course, not every kid has a game system or a PC joystick, but it's getting awfully close. A national survey of 500 parents found that 9 out of 10 said their kids owned or rented games in 1998.

All those new games are just irresistible to the kids who hold the controllers. "It's the first thing Ricky and David do when they get home on Friday or wake up on the weekends," says Mom, Mindy Picone. The Picones limit game time to weekends, but many kids don't have to play by such rules. In fact, 1 out of 7 kids who play video and computer games plays at least an hour and a half a day, according to psychologist David Walsh of the National Institute on Media and the Family. Then there's the hard core 7% who play three or more hours a day!

Are Kids Addicted?

You know the kids. The ones who spend more time playing Zelda or Pokeman than eating or sleeping. They prefer video-game playing to any other activity. They get angry when they can't play.

"There's this one kid," says John Szendiuch, 12, of Pelham, New York, "it's his whole life. He walks around the lunchroom with his Game Boy saying, 'Wanna battle? Wanna trade?' I think he's definitely addicted."

When kids become obsessed, parents get upset. Ron Hughes, 38, of Bridgeton, Missouri, found that he couldn't even talk to his son Russell, 9, because the boy was so absorbed in Pokemon. "The phone would ring," says Hughes, "and Russell wouldn't hear it."

Parents are also worried about the violence. The blood and gore gushing from games like Duke Nukem: Time to Kill and Resident Evil are enough to make some parents ban all video games from their home.

What's Good about Games?

Surprisingly, experts who study kids and video games say the games are not all bad as long as kids don't go overboard. Patricia M. Greenfield, a California psychology professor, believes that games are one reason for the increase in intelligence-test scores since the 1970s. "They raise nonverbal thinking skills and visual intelligence," she says.

David Walsh agrees. He says games, such as Tetris and the Carmen San Diego series, "engage and entertain the mind while introducing puzzle-solving skills."

Some kids are convinced that controlling a joystick and firing video weapons help improve their hand-eye coordination. Nice try, but research does not back this up. Hitting a button on a controller, says Walsh, will help you get better at just that skill: hitting a button on your controller.

Are games addictive? Only in the sense that "all fun is addictive," says child psychologist Robert Butterworth of Los Angeles. Still, there's no denying that when you've been playing Zelda for an hour and you've finally found your way out of the Spirit Temple, or you're playing Pokemon and you're about to capture Charmander, it's just about impossible to quit—even though dinner's on the table.

Time's Up

How do you avoid battles over video games? "It's important for parents to take an interest in what kids are playing," says Walsh. Then they can make reasonable rules and maybe even understand what kids love about the games.

Butterworth says he plays Nintendo 64 with his son Anton, 13. "He whups me. He just blows me away!" Still, both Butterworth and Walsh believe parents must limit kids' playing time. Walsh recommends no more than 90 minutes a day.

But watch out. Such limits are about to become harder to enforce. This spring Sega will unveil Sega Dreamcast. It has a 128-bit processor, so it will be twice as sharp and clear as a Nintendo 64. PlayStation's own 128-bit player will be out next year. Everything that makes video games amazing and attractive to kids will be getting bigger, brighter and more irresistible than ever.

—*TIME For Kids*

Appendix C: Sources for Alternative Model Texts

IF YOU'RE LOOKING for alternative model texts to use in the conferences in *Strategic Writing Conferences*, here are a few places to begin your search:

Personal Narrative and Memoir

One of my favorite sources for these personal narratives and memoirs is the books that children's literature authors have written about their childhoods. Many of the chapters in these books work as great model texts:

▶ Greenfield, Eloise. *Childtimes.*
▶ Little, Jean. *Little by Little.*
▶ Meyers, Walter Dean. *Bad Boy.*
▶ Sleator, William. *Oddballs.*
▶ Spinelli, Jerry. *Knots in My Yo-Yo String: The Autobiography of a Kid.*

You'll find many picture books that fit into the personal narrative and memoir genres, as well. Look for books like *Saturdays and Teacakes* by Lester Laminack that focus on a special event in the author's childhood.

The *Chicken Soup* books (*Chicken Soup for the Kid's Soul,* etc.) also contain wonderful personal narratives and memoirs that are useful in conferences.

Short Story

My favorite sources of short fiction are children's magazines. *Highlights* and *Cricket Magazine* are two especially good sources of high-interest, well-written short fiction for children. *Stone Soup* and *Merlyn's Pen* contain student-written short fiction of very high quality.

You'll also find numerous collections of short fiction for children in your school or public library and local bookstore. Some collections are written by a single author, such as Cynthia Rylant's *Every Living Thing;* others contain stories written by several authors, such as the books edited by Donald Gallo for adolescents.

Feature Article

Start your search for feature articles in some of these children's magazines:

▶ *American Girl*
▶ *Boys' Life*
▶ *Ranger Rick*
▶ *TIME For Kids*

You'll also find numerous feature articles in newspapers, especially in the sections that aren't devoted to that day's news. Some newspapers have a weekly kid section that contains high-interest feature articles for children.

Op-Ed

For op-eds (opinion-editorial pieces) about subjects your students will know something about and be opinionated about, the best source is your local newspaper. Look for op-eds that focus on local and regional issues. *USA Today* is a national newspaper in which I find a lot of op-eds that can be used with children.

Personal Essay

You'll sometimes find examples of personal essays in the newspaper, usually in the "Life" section. For example, *USA Today* regularly publishes personal essays. And many newspapers publish personal essays around holidays, such as Mother's Day or Father's Day.

Newsweek publishes a personal essay penned by a guest writer in the "My Life" section.

Additional Sources

Many of the educators who have written books about writing workshop curriculum discuss their favorite sources of model texts. One of the best of these discussions is contained in Katie Wood Ray's *Study Driven: A Framework for Planning Units of Study in the Writing Workshop,* in which she lists sources for all of the above-mentioned genres, as well as for many others.

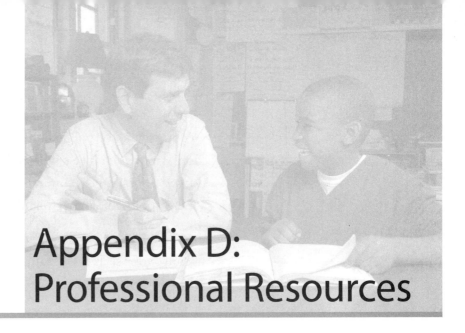

Appendix D: Professional Resources

Anderson, Carl. 2005. *Assessing Writers.* Portsmouth, NH: Heinemann.

Anderson, Carl. 2000. *How's it Going? A Practical Guide to Conferring with Student Writers.* Portsmouth, NH: Heinemanan.

Anderson, Jeff. 2005. *Mechanically Inclined: Building Grammar, Usage, and Style into Writer's Workshop.* Portland, ME: Stenhouse Publishers.

Anderson, Jeff. 2007. *Everyday Editing: Inviting Students to Develop Skill and Craft in Writer's Workshop.* Portland, ME: Stenhouse Publishers.

Angelillo, Janet. 2002. *A Fresh Approach to Teaching Punctuation.* New York: Scholastic.

Angelillo, Janet. 2005. *Making Revision Matter: Strategies for Guiding Students to Focus, Organize, and Strengthen Their Writing Independently.* New York: Scholastic.

Angelillo, Janet. 2008. *Grammar Study.* New York: Scholastic.

Atwell, Nancie. 1998. *In the Middle: New Understandings about Writing, Reading, and Learning.* Portsmouth, NH: Heinemann.

Bomer, Katherine. 2005. *Writing a Life: Teaching Memoir to Sharpen Insight, Shape Meaning—And Triumph Over Tests.* Portsmouth, NH: Heinemann.

Bomer, Katherine, and Randy Bomer. 2001. *For a Better World: Reading and Writing for Social Action.* Portsmouth, NH: Heinemann.

Bomer, Randy. 1995. *Time for Meaning: Crafting Literate Lives in Middle & High School.* Portsmouth, NH: Heinemann.

Buckner, Aimee. 2005. *Notebook Know-How: Strategies for the Writer's Notebook.* Portland, ME: Stenhouse Publishers.

Calkins, Lucy. 1994. *The Art of Teaching Writing.* Portsmouth, NH: Heinemann.

Calkins, Lucy, and Marjorie Martinelli, Ted Kesler, Cory Gillette, Medea McEvoy, Mary Chiarella, M. Colleen Cruz. 2006. *Units of Study for Teaching Writing, Grades 3–5.* Portsmouth, NH: Heinemann.

Calkins, Lucy and Pat Bleichman, Amanda Hartman, Natalie Louis, Leah Mermelstein, Abby Oxenhorn, Stephanie Parsons, Laurie Pessah. 2003. *Units of Study for Primary Writing: A Yearlong Curriculum.* Portsmouth, NH: Heinemann.

Calkins, Lucy, and M. Colleen Cruz. 2006. *Writing Fiction: Big Dreams, Tall Ambitions.* Portsmouth, NH: Heinemann.

Calkins, Lucy, and Cory Gillette. 2006. *Breathing Life into Essays.* Portsmouth, NH: Heinemann.

Calkins, Lucy, and Shelley Harwayne. 1990. *Living Between the Lines.* Portsmouth, NH: Heinemann.

Cruz, M. Colleen. 2004. *Independent Writing: One Teacher—Thirty-Two Needs, Topics, and Plans.* Portsmouth, NH: Heinemann.

Davis, Judy, and Sharon Hill. 2003. *The No-Nonsense Guide to Teaching Writing: Strategies,*

Structures, and Solutions. Portsmouth, NH: Heinemann.

Dolch, E.W. (1948). *Problems in Reading.* Champaign, IL: Garrard Press.

Ehrenworth, Mary, and Vicki Vinton. 2005. *The Power of Grammar.* Portsmouth, NH: Heinemann.

Feigelson, Dan. 2008. *Practical Punctuation: Lessons on Rule Making and Rule Breaking in Elementary Writing.* Portsmouth, NH: Heinemann.

Fletcher, Ralph. 1993. *What a Writer Needs.* Portsmouth, NH: Heinemann.

Fletcher, Ralph. 1996. *Breathing In, Breathing Out.* Portsmouth, NH: Heinemann.

Fletcher, Ralph. 2006. *Boy Writers: Reclaiming Their Voices.* Portland, ME: Stenhouse Publishers.

Fletcher, Ralph, and JoAnn Portalupi. *Lessons for the Writer's Notebook.* Portsmouth, NH: Heinemann.

Graves, Donald. 1994. *A Fresh Look at Writing.* Portsmouth, NH: Heinemann.

Graves, Donald. 2003. *Writing: Teachers and Children at Work.* Twentieth-Anniversary Edition. Portsmouth, NH: Heinemann.

Heard, Georgia. 2002. *The Revision Toolbox: Teaching Techniques That Work.* Portsmouth, NH: Heinemann.

Lane, Barry. 1992. *After THE END: Teaching and Learning Creative Revision.* Portsmouth, NH: Heinemann.

Murray, Donald. 2004. *Write to Learn,* 8th ed. Boston, MA: Wadsworth Publishing.

Newkirk, Thomas. 2002. *Misreading Masculinity: Boys, Literacy, and Popular Culture.* Portsmouth, NH: Heinemann.

Ray, Katie Wood. 1999. *Wondrous Words: Writers and Writing in the Elementary Classroom.* Urbana, IL: National Council of Teachers of English.

Ray, Katie Wood. 2006. *Study Driven: A Framework for Planning Units of Study in the Writing Workshop.* Portsmouth, NH: Heinemann.

Romano, Tom. 2004. *Crafting Authentic Voice.* Portsmouth, NH: Heinemann.

Smith, Frank. 1988. *Joining the Literacy Club: Further Essays into Education.* Portsmouth, NH: Heinemann.

Strong, William. 1999. "Coaching Writing Development: Syntax Revisited, Options Explored." In *Evaluating Writing: The Role of Teachers' Knowledge about Text, Learning, and Culture,* edited by Charles R. Cooper and Lee Odell, 72–92. Urbana, IL: NCTE.

Weaver, Connie. 1996. *Teaching Grammar in Context.* Portsmouth, NH: Heinemann.

Zinsser, William. 2006. *On Writing Well: The Classic Guide to Writing Nonfiction,* 30th ed. New York: HarperCollins.

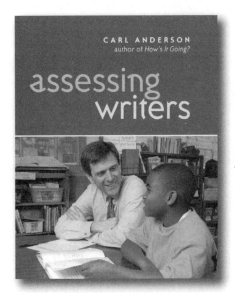